QUICKIES

(Don't you just love Quickies)

QUICKIES

(Don't you just love Quickies)

Don P. Marquess

To order additional copies of this book, contact:
Xlibris
844-714-8691
www.Xlibris.com
Orders@Xlibris.com
830544

CONTENTS

PREFACE

As I write this, I am almost eighty years of age. With any luck at all, I will make it. All of the stories in this "Quickies" book are real-life experiences with no names changed in any way whatsoever. I have not attempted to protect the innocent. Why would an innocent person care anyway? Probably most of the people mentioned in this book have long since passed away and therefore can't refute nor complain about their names being used in this book, and the others would be disinclined to purchase this book anyway. I have loved telling these stories for years, with urging of those who listened to them and apparently enjoyed them, I have been encouraged to put them in print. I have been told by several physicians and a few brainiacs that I have an eidetic memory, which is a "near-photographic" memory, so all of these stories are exactly as I remember them. I researched these from the recesses of my mind. And these stories have been researched for accuracy and verified by me. They are all written just as I speak them.

These Quickies are presented in the hope that after a hard day at work or a difficult day doing nothing, these true-life stories will bring a smile to the readers' face.

My close friend, the late Rich Wolfe, writer of over fifty books, who used my photos on the covers of five of his books (four with my permission), all best sellers, termed my writings "Thurberesque" in homage to James Thurber. My stories are short and do not take a major commitment to read. They are sort of like *The Far Side*

Cartoons by Gary Larson. Read them, smile, and then turn to the sports page. Think Max Shulman and Jean Shepherd.

Also, I was encouraged to write all of these stories by the noted child psychiatrist, David Berland, MD, since my stories are somewhat childish in their simplicity.

The world's most honored professor of the piccolo, Jan Gippo, who wrote the bible of piccoloists, *The Complete Piccolo*, was on the faculty of Webster University and is currently teaching at the University of Missouri in Kansas City, and is also an avid reader, who strongly encouraged me to put these stories in print. Jan loves a great story but also possesses an inability to remember punch lines.

I completed seven projects with Jack Buck, the Hall of Fame broadcaster, who every Saturday morning in his kitchen had me laughing at his sophistication in telling humorous anecdotes. Jack, in his later years, became a very prolific poet, and we incorporated his poems onto my photos. I spent many weekend mornings with him as he read his latest poem that would end up on one of my photos. Jack was a major source of my baseball-related stories.

There are stories that mention encounters with Burt Reynolds, Henry Mancini, and a few other celebrities of note. All of these stories are absolutely true-life stories that have occurred in my (almost) eighty years.

Hopefully, you will read them and enjoy doing so . . . but keep the sports page handy.

ERIC AND TRACEY TAVENER

Susan and I had been married for four months or so when she concocted this caper. Susan, by the way, was the most beautiful and intelligent person I ever met. She resembled a gorgeous combination of Barbara Feldon (Agent 99 in *Get Smart*), Marlo Thomas, and Cher, and she also possessed a delightful and devilish sense of humor. We were watching an old movie on TV called "After the Thin Man," or one of the six or seven versions with the same Nick and Nora Charles (William Powell and Myrna Loy) when Susan said that she thought the two of us could be private investigators. She even had our alias created. We would be Eric and Tracey Tavener. (She had apparently been harboring such thoughts for some time, because the names she mentioned were far too good to have been a spontaneous creation.) I immediately warmed to the idea and had thoughts that the Tavener Agency had a very reliable and distinguished sound.

I said, "Susan, that sounds great. However, neither one of us has any experience whatsoever. We need more than just a great sounding name for our private investigating firm. We don't even know how to secretly spy on anyone, much less tail anyone while being unnoticed." Herein is the origin of the caper.

Our apartment was in General Grant Colonial Village, a development that for a newlywed couple was just the most glorious complex we could imagine. (In reality, it was just nice, but to us, being newlyweds and goofy in love, it was absolute heaven.) It was named after the Civil War general whose farm was within shouting distance of the apartment complex. Also, the complex was in a slightly different direction of shouting distance from a very shady motel named "Coral Courts" that had a sign in front advertising "hourly rates." It also had individual cabins with single car parking garages with overhead doors to the units. We needed some experience in tailing someone without detections, so we decided to go there and kind of lurk in the shadows on the parking lot of the Marlboro Lanes Bowling Alley next to Coral Courts. We waited and huddled in the car with the engine and headlights off. We knew that anyone leaving there at 10:30 p.m. or so on a Friday night had probably been up to no good. Shortly, our thoughts materialized. We waited for fifteen minutes or so, then . . .

A white Eldorado Cadillac was leaving Coral Courts. In the passenger's seat was a woman with platinum blond hair. The driver was wearing a white hat with a black band. We imagined that he also had a pencil-thin mustache and a pinky ring, and probably looked very sleazy.

Susan, gleeful as she could be, said, "Let's get him."

So we waited until he left the motel driveway and turned left on the major Watson Road thoroughfare. Quietly and very stealthily, we started our pursuit. We lagged back, knowing that the Taveners were undetected. We continued behind, following a very safe one hundred or so yards behind. This was a great idea, and it was working. The Cadillac continued east to Jamieson Avenue and turned right, so we did the same, still knowing that we were invisible to our "perp." He turned left on Eichelberger Street, then went two blocks, and turned left. We laid back and did the same. He drove around Francis Park, and so did we, traveling safely behind. Then, when we saw the car again, we saw no blond in the front seat, and the driver accelerated very quickly. We assumed that he had discovered our tail, told the blond to duck down in the front seat (or maybe threw her out), and was going to elude our pursuit. We would have none of that. He took a right, then another right, and we were closer behind him. Then he turned left on Eichelberger and had upped his speed to 50 mph or so. We were unrelenting and did the same. He sped across Hampton Avenue (another major thoroughfare), and we were right behind, closer to him than ever. He saw an alleyway and turned on to it at his increased speed. I slowed up and didn't continue the pursuit.

Susan yelled and said, "He's getting away, why are you stopping?"

I said, "Susan, for God's sake, what will we do if we catch him?"

For the first time in a while, she was silent. Fortunately, we came to our senses and ended the chase. We both felt, however, that that man lived in fear for several days wondering who was pursuing him. I felt that he probably anticipated a wifely confrontation for a goodly (or badly) amount of time. Our foray into the private detective business failed, although we probably caused a man to live in fear for a while.

George C. Cockerel, May He Rest in Peace

It was a somewhat sultry Sunday in August as Don Flaskamper and I exited the cool air-conditioning of the Redbirds Lanes Bowling Alley and stepped into the hot humid typical St. Louis summer breeze. As we were leaving the parking lot in my daddy's '56 mandarin orange and white Ford Victoria, we passed the rear of the Lucisic Monuments building where there were dumped and discarded tombstones. We supposed that the names were misspelled or the date of departure was incorrect or some other flaw that had to be reengraved. There in the discarded pile of headstones was a large stone with the name George C. Cockerel who died in 1953. This was in 1958, so we figured he had been dead long enough to not catch us lifting his monument. It was somewhat strange that Don and I thought the same thing at the same time. That tombstone was ours!! We also had the same idea what we were going to do with it.

There were a group of guys that hung around together in high school. Actually, I was an outsider in the group (which highly inventively was called "The Group") due to the fact that I was Catholic and went to a private high school, while the rest of the group were heathens and went to a public high school. The oldest of this group (by several months) of five guys was Roger Goessling, a six-foot-five-inch 140 pounder. Tall and skinny, Roger who could devour six or seven Big Bevos in a single sitting. (In 1958, Big Macs had not hit the St. Louis market, but a restaurant named Schneithorst's had their version named the "Big Bevo.") At any rate, Roger, the tall and skinny, was not with us that afternoon, so he was the perfect candidate for our caper. We knew we were going to use that tombstone for a delightfully sinister prank.

We lifted that extremely heavy headstone into the trunk of the orange Victoria, and it made a resounding *thump* when it hit the trunk floor. We drove off to get the proper tools—two shovels and a bushel basket—so we could borrow (steal) dirt from a local construction site. Remember, this was a Sunday afternoon and no construction was going on. We filled the bushel basket to overflowing with dirt, placed it in the trunk next to good ol' George C., and headed to the rear of the florist shop. We assumed that the florists did the same as the monument folks did and threw dead or moldy flowers in the trash in the backs of their buildings. We were right, a florist in our neighborhood had done just that, and we gathered three dozen or so slightly and greatly withered red roses from the alley in the rear of the shop. We then had all of the necessary ingredients for our project.

It was almost seven o'clock at this time, so it was getting dark, not very dark but just dark enough not to be easily seen but yet light enough to see what we were going to do. We drove to the alley behind Roger's house, opened the trunk, and struggled to take out the headstone. Don and I were both strong kids, but this damn thing was heavy, probably close to three hundred pounds. We lifted it out and took baby steps to place it in the perfect spot in Roger's backyard, placing it facing east so the morning sun would illuminate it adoringly. We brought the bushel basket of dirt and mounded it nicely in front of the tombstone just like it was a freshly dug grave. And then, just like the cartoon cat, Sylvester, we tiptoed our way back to the grave and placed the flowers. The red roses were the finishing touch, and it was a glorious sight.

Now, a freshly dug grave in one's backyard must conjure up many thoughts, none of which are fun. First of all, is it a real grave? A frightening thought at best. Also, why would someone bury someone in a private backyard? All of these thoughts were absolutely delicious, anticipating the wonderful reactions of one discovering a freshly dug grave in their backyard. We got into our orange hearse and quietly drove away.

The next morning, I received a call from our fish, Roger, the tall and skinny. He said that he was just waking up and he heard his mother from their bedroom say, "Gus, there is a grave in our backyard".

Gus then responded, "Go back to sleep, Edith."

"No, Gus, there really is a grave in our backyard." Roger said he heard his father's feet hit the floor and then a long pause. Then he heard both of them in unison yell, *"Roger!"*

Don and I were both reprimanded by our parents, but my mom and dad kept laughing when they told me what a hideous thing I had done.

LOBSTER, ANYONE?

Susan was born in New Jersey. She lived first in Woodbridge and then Woodbury, but always close to the Atlantic Ocean beaches. At least much closer to the Atlantic Ocean than a landlubber like me, being only from a river city, St. Louis, and miles and several days from either ocean. Susan, being so close to the ocean, thought of lobster and crab legs not as delicacies but just staples of lunch and dinner fare. I always felt that if anyone wanted to entice her, they could just drag a lobster behind them and she would follow them anywhere.

There is a seafood specialist grocer in St. Louis called Bob's Seafood that features live lobster and crab. I called them and asked for the largest live lobster he had in the tank. Bob said that he had a six-and-a-half pounder that was just ripe for steaming. This was Christmas Eve and I thought it would make a delightful surprise gift for "Lobster Susan." I bought it and had it packed in a box with seaweed. It was a very alive and active lobster and it kept popping the lid of the box on my drive home. This was Christmas Eve in St. Louis and the temperature was in the mid-thirties. We had an unheated garage, which was just perfect for storing the gift lobster.

I thought, what the hell, why not wrap it up as a gift and place it under the tree? I found the perfect shade of lobster red shiny paper and wrapped the live lobster box, leaving an open section in the wrapping so in the morning when I came downstairs to light the tree, it would be easy to seal the box while Susan and our two boys waited at the top of the stairs for me to say, "Santa came, come on down." I placed a big red satin bow on the box, sealed it, and added a tag that said, "For Susan . . . Open me first." I then gave the all clear, and Susan, Donny, and Danny came downstairs to view the wonders that Santa delivered. Susan and I decided that Santa would always only get credit for three unwrapped gifts that he usually brought. All of the other gifts were wrapped with their individual name tags saying, "From Mom and Dad."

I led Susan to the brightly lit and sparkling seven-foot Christmas tree and pointed to the box marked "Open Me First." Susan usually shakes a package and tries to determine what is in it before she unwraps it, which she did so this time wondering what could be so loose inside to be moving around so much. Her curiosity caused her to think maybe it was a jewelry box that I had wrapped in a bigger box, so she proceeded to unwrap it. Just when she was about to take the lid off, all the shaking awakened the lobster, and he was one mad crustacean. A giant claw shot out of the box, and Susan screamed and dropped the box. The lobster, one big fellow, fell on the floor, with Donny and Danny screaming and Susan laughing and screaming at the same time. It was indeed a challenge to capture the wild and maniacal lobster, but finally we got him! Our boys named the lobster "Ozzie," making it very difficult for Susan to cook something that had a name. Nevertheless, her appetite for lobster overcame her aversion to cooking a named animal, and we had that delicious "Ozzie" for dinner. The boys had no problem dipping the named morsels in the freshly drawn butter.

Just as an afterstatement, Susan, who cooked many a lobster, said that the more humane way of cooking one is, rather than placing the lobster in a boiling pot, which she said causes the lobster to stiffen and become tough, she put the lobster in a moderately warm pot and slowly raised the heat, lulling the lobster into a calm restful death. What a supremely humane method of dealing death to something edible. She was right, Ozzie was tender and delicious.

While on the Christmas subject, from the time I was eight or nine years old, around the middle of November, I became my grandmother's cookie sous-chef. (At eight years old, I just thought I was her helper. I learned the sous-chef term much later in life.) My grandmom was easily the greatest cookie baker on the planet, and it was a great adventure to assist in the creation of those delicious gems. She made date/walnut cookies, pfeffernuss cookies which were some old German recipe (where my grandmother got it was questionable because she was all English and Irish without a trace of German), rum balls (I was not allowed to actively participate in the creation of those), some sort of licorice cookies which she called "Annie's cookies" (I learned later that these were anise cookies), and my favorite of all, her world-famous Scotch shortbread butter cookies, which I guess were immediate artery cloggers but nevertheless delicious. Toward the end of the batch of those, she let me roll out the leftover dough and make whatever shape and size I wanted. With my great creative abilities at that time of my life, they ended up as strange trapezoidal shapes of two to three bite sizes. My grandmom usually baked twenty dozen or so of each kind, so all members of our families could gorge on them until our buttons gave way and rocketed off. It was these great cookie memories that got me to implore the world's second-best cookie maker, my wife Susan, to make Christmas cookies. She kept delaying the baking of those, and I was getting anxious.

I was at the Missouri Botanical Gardens gift shop one afternoon and saw a spindle with various Christmas cards. One that particularly caught my eye was a card with a sweet-looking bear wearing an apron, a "Mother Hubbard" lacy hat, and holding a plate full of Christmas cookies. The bear's head was slightly tilted to the side and had a sweet grin on her face. Inside of the card was some sort of cheery message that I can't remember, but I signed the card saying, "Enough of this sweet Christmas drivel, *where are my cookies*?" I left that card leaning against the coffeepot as I left for work that morning.

I came home after work and opened the front door, and there was Susan wearing a Mother Hubbard hat, a burnt orange turtleneck sweater, and an apron. She was holding a plate of freshly baked cookies, had her head tilted slightly, and had a sweet smile on her beautiful face. She was a perfect replica of the card that I left for her that morning. She turned around and she was *totally naked* from the waist down.

Dinner and cookies that evening had a delightful delay!

The Evening That Almost Ruined Our Lives

There was a bowling alley named Arway Lanes, which was on Arsenal Street just west of Kingshighway Boulevard that was a very popular bowling establishment. "The Group," which was Dave Twist, Roger Goessling, Don Flaskamper, Ronnie Thoen, and yours truly, Don Marquess, decided to join a bowling league because we had a secret weapon . . . David Twist was a bowler on the "Little Budweisers." There was a bowling team called "The Budweisers," and if I remember correctly, Don Carter and Ray Blueth were on that team. It was a terrific team that won a lot. The "Little Budweisers" were formed by sons of Budweiser employees. Dave Twist's father was a brewmaster for Anheuser-Busch, so Dave became a member of that team. The "Little Budweisers" had five excellent bowlers, and our good friend and member of The Group was on the team. With Dave as the anchor on our team, we were golden!

Before the term "designated driver" was coined, I became one. Apparently, I wasn't born with the alcohol gene since neither of my parents ever drank. I think there was one bottle of alcohol in our house for the first eighteen years of my life until one night a guest dealt death to it, declaring "good old Guckenheimer ish besh ebber." The fact that I am a teetotaler is due to no great moral conviction, but due to the fact that I hate the taste of alcohol and I have a definite allergy to it. One sip and my lips get numb, and I have a brain-chilling pain right above my eyebrows, therefore, I don't drink at all. The rest of our team did, however.

We, as expected, were ruling our league since Dave Twist was carrying a 237 average. The rest of us carried 180s (except for me, I struggled to keep above 160), so we blew away all the other contending teams in the league . . . except for one night. Dave Twist, the magnificent, bowled 135 his first game. Unheard of!

Dave was livid (actually, I think his color was a light magenta) and he had several beers in him as he stated, "If I don't roll 210 my next game, I am taking my bowling ball and rolling it down Arsenal Avenue!"

This was a ridiculous statement, and we all knew it. This was a Friday night and Arway Lanes was on Arsenal just above one of the busiest streets in St. Louis, and traffic was very heavy this time of night. However, we all felt comfortable that he would bowl over 210 his next game. He didn't. He barely made 200.

I should have known better since I was the only totally sober one of our team, but no, I was almost the premier taunter, saying, "Come on, Dave, let's see that old black beauty roll down Arsenal Street."

The other three team members had enough beer to cajole him into that stupid action. The bowling alley was on a street on a hill that led to a stoplight on the corner of Kingshighway, so the bowling ball would roll easily into that intersection. We all almost pushed Dave to fulfill his promise and went to the middle of Arsenal Street. Dave, with his usual approach, full of style and determination, took his ball and let it fly. *Egad*! As the ball started rolling, it gained speed and started to bounce in the air, first one foot and then two, gaining speed and height as it rolled toward Kingshighway. We all thought our lives were over as that sixteen-pound cannonball was surely going to smash the windshield of oncoming traffic on that very busy thoroughfare and kill several people. There is no way to stop a galloping bowling ball.

Fortunately, the light for Kingshighway traffic turned red, and it was like Moses parting the Red Sea. The ball bounced higher and higher across Kingshighway, split into two pieces, and landed in the corner of Tower Grove Park just across the intersection. *No cars hit!* Apparently, no one even noticed because no cars stopped with people getting out of their cars and looking for the bowling-ball halves, so we all went back into the bowling alley and played the third game. Dave just grabbed a ball from the rental rack and rolled a very respectable 231.

I don't think we all realized (at that moment at least) just how fortunate we all were that the light changed when it did. I could be writing this from my prison cell!

Jack Buck, My Partner & Friend

It may have been 1970 and the Cardinals starting pitcher may have been Reggie Cleveland, but, at the moment that is irrelevant. What is very relevant is Jack Buck was broadcasting the game. The

Cardinals pitcher walked the first batter on four pitches and Jack Buck gave his traditional opening after the first batter by saying "And that's the way this one starts". Then the next batter walked on five pitches. The next batter walked on six pitches loading the bases. The fourth batter walked on five pitches walking in the first run of the game. Jack said, "What an ignominious way to start a ball game!". It was then I realized that he was not the ordinary play by play announcer. He was indeed a highly sophisticated wordsmith.

I grew up listening to Harry Caray and his unique way of calling a game. Harry Caray could make a pop foul very exciting. If you tuned in the game in the later innings, you could just tell by the tone in Harry's voice whether the Cardinals were winning or losing. Many people thought he was the best ever, and many fans felt they were more Harry Caray fans than Cardinals fans. When Jack Buck became his partner is 1954, most people just thought of him as a rather nondescript shadow in the booth with Harry. How wrong they were.

Ron Jacober, Sports Director for KMOX, told me this story about a game at Wrigley against the Cubs. It was "Teen Night" and after the game there was to be a rock band playing with dancing in the aisles. During the game both Harry and Jack commented about one teen couple in the stands paying much more attention to each other than the game. In the middle of the third inning, Harry Caray said to Jack "I have been watching them throughout this game and I figured it out, he kisses her on the strikes and she kisses him on the balls!". Ron Jacober said that Jack Buck looked at Harry in total disbelief of what he said. Ron said that Jack's expression personified the word "incredulity". Harry then realized what he said, started laughing, pushed the "cough button" and pointed to Jack to continue. There was no way Jack could contain his laughter, pushed his cough button and pointed to Harry for him to continue. Dead Air ensued. The game was still progressing with neither of the announcers able to continue saying anything. Ron Jacober told me that in the middle of that inning with only one out, they broke for a commercial....a really long commercial break. The next inning started, and Harry was still laughing and pointed to Jack to take over, he couldn't, so they broke for another commercial. Then the mikes went live again with one out in the top of the fourth when Jack finally takes the mike and says to Harry Caray "Why don't we just talk about what is going on in the game?".

Jack Buck broadcasted for the Cardinals for forty-seven years and captured the hearts of Cardinal Nation. He could have run for mayor and won in a landslide. Many prominent celebrities, if one was fortunate enough to meet one, really were somewhat distant when you were talking to them, and you got the feeling that they were in "program mode" and not really looking at you, nor caring about you....but not Jack Buck. He seemed as interested in you as you were in him. He would always ask your name, where you were from, and what you were doing. Jack never turned down a request for an autograph or a few words of conversation. He was not only a gentleman, but a very considerate person who made you feel that he felt fortunate to meet you.

I met Jack due to my baseball art photography, and he also interviewed me several times, regarding a new photo I produced, on his dugout show prior to games. We, the entire Marty Hendin gang, including Fredbird, my wife, Susan, and I, were at JBuck's Restaurant in Clayton, MO celebrating my 60th birthday when Jack came into our private room and started telling jokes and making everyone laugh. My celebration was indeed a great one. He then recited a poem that he had just written about baseball. It was titled "365", which meant that if you were a baseball fan, you were thinking about baseball every day of the year, and baseball was usually uppermost in your thoughts, whether during the season or not. It was a great poem and everyone loved it. For me there are only two sports seasons... baseball, and the off season, so I truly related to his poem.

Susan and I went on the Cardinals Cruise every year and on the cruise after my birthday, Marty Hendin read Jack's "365" poem and the entire theater (all Cardinals Fans) gave it a standing ovation. When we got back to St. Louis, I called Jack and told him about the reception his poem received and that we should produce it and offer it for sale. I had taken a photo of his bronze statue right after sculptor Harry Weber produced it and I told Jack that we should incorporate his poem on that photo and offer it to his fans. Jack loved the idea, and we went in partnership in the project.

Since it was for profit, and not for charity, Jack felt he couldn't promote it himself on the air as it would be using his airtime for personal profit, so he arranged several interviews for me to speak about it. The Cardinals flagship station, KMOX, had a very successful hour long show in prime time called "Sports Open Line" hosted by Randy Karraker, and Jack arranged for me to be on the show. I thought it would be just for a few minutes, but I was on for the entire hour show. (Which probably amounted to $10,000 or so in free advertising)

During my appearance on the show Randy Karraker while looking at the Print with Jack's sculpture and the poem said, "There is a red background on the print and at the stadium and there is no red background, it is just a concrete block wall, how did you do that?" I responded, "I got the statue before it's erection and photographed it with a red cloth backdrop". Randy commented that it really looked great. Later in the show, I once again stated that "I got the statue before it's erection", which was grammatically correct.

I had left my phone in the car and after the show I went to my car and the call screen said I had missed thirteen calls. The first one was from my wife Susan who said, "Oh Jack is going to be so proud with everyone driving by that statue to see his erection!" It then dawned on me what I had said. Another of the calls was from my friend, Jan Gippo who said "It's ERECTION? It's ERECTION?....and you said it TWICE!!. Boy oh boy, you got a great opportunity on the number one station in St. Louis, and you really messed it up!" The rest of the calls had the similar message, except for one of my friends who said "Nice interview".

After that photo project, Jack and I became partners in six more of projects of incorporating his poems onto my photos. Every print we produced sold very well. Jack was an outstanding broadcaster and in his last few years of life he became a very prolific and quite masterful poet. Jack was a major patriot and had a Purple Heart from WWII, and many of his poems reflected that patriotism. Perhaps one of his finest poems written was after September 11, 2001 when the Twin

Towers were destroyed and 2,800 people lost their lives. After that tragedy all life seemed to stop. Baseball ceased play, as did every other sport and entertainment activity. America was stunned, and joy and happiness were missing from the lives of all Americans. Baseball took a one-week absence. The Cardinals game was the first game to return, which was an afternoon game carried nationally on ESPN. Before the game started, Jack Buck stood at home plate in Busch Stadium and said, "Many people wonder if it is time for baseball to return…I think we have the answer!". 44,000 stood and cheered. Jack Buck read the poem he wrote, and afterwards, the Lee Greenwood song "Proud to be an American" was played. You have heard this saying before, but there wasn't a dry eye in 40,000 plus fans.

Jack wrote a poem titled "What Would the World be without Music" for the St. Louis Symphony for the opening evening of their fund-raising season. It was to be a Black-Tie Event and Jack was the Master of Ceremonies. He asked me to print the poem for him and I found an old, yellowed music script and incorporated his poem on it. I gave it to Jack and he thought it looked terrific. I had gotten to think of Jack as my friend, as he could always make me laugh. He looked at my print of his poem and thought it was beautiful and then asked what the music behind the poem was. I said, "Jack, it is an early version of "Roll Me Over In The Clover". He laughed. It was then that I thought he thought of me as his friend also. Jack read that poem at Powell Hall and presented it to the Symphony for hanging in their administrative offices.

I have a very close friend with the St. Louis Symphony who has been their piccoloist (the guy who plays the piccolo) for 35 years or so named Jan (pronounced Yahn) Gippo who was present at the opening and asked me if it was possible to get Jack to sign one for the musicians of the symphony to hang in the lobby of Powell Hall. I asked Jack and he said, "Of course, also print one for you and Susan, and another one for Carole (Jack's wife)". I had them printed the next day and had them with me in my car to bring to Jack the following Saturday.

One Saturday morning at Jack's in his kitchen, I mentioned a Yogi Berra Quote that I thought was really funny regarding his remarking about a restaurant and saying, "Nobody goes there anymore, it's too crowded". Jack said that he felt that most of the Yogi quotes were massaged by the media to make them even funnier. But he said he knew two things that Yogi actually said, because Yogi said them to Jack. Jack said that the Astros (Yogi was a coach for them) had just finished a series with the Dodgers on the West Coast, and the Cardinals had just finished a series in New York with the Mets. The cardinals and the Astros were meeting in Houston for a series. Jack said that in the corridor of the Astrodome he and Yogi met, they had the usual Hi's, and handshakes, when Yogi said to Jack, "When did you get here?" Jack replied, "Oh about an hour ago". Yogi said, "East Coast Time or Central Time?" Jack said he could think of no way to respond to that. The other time that Jack said Yogi truly said a Yogi ism was when they were both in Cooperstown going to a welcoming celebrity dinner. Yogi was on the bus when Jack got on, saw Yogi, and asked him, "Yogi, what time is it?" Yogi said, "You mean right now?" Once again, Jack was speechless.

Two of Yogi's statements that I know are true because I heard them both in the "This Week in Baseball Show" with Mel Allen being the host. Yogi, who at the time was a coach for the Mets, was asked by Mel Allen about the poor attendance at the Mets games. Yogi responded by saying, "If fans don't want to come to our games, how are you going to stop them?" In the very same interview Yogi said (being the true sage he was) "In baseball there are ONLY good times and bad times, and THIS is not one of those times."

I had the very fortunate honor of being the only art photographer to photograph and produce prints of Mark McGwire's 70th home run baseball. I have a multi-page document giving me those exclusive art photographic rights. The sports attorney, Michael Barnes, arranged for me to also photograph Sammy Sosa's 66th home run baseball. Sammy's 66th homerun ball was flown to St. Louis and I photographed it. I had arrived at Jack Buck's home for a meeting one afternoon when Michael Barnes called and said that he would be offering a contract to whoever caught Barry Bonds 71st home run baseball and wanted me, probably for continuity, to photograph that ball in a contract similar to the one I had for McGwire's and Sosa's record-breaking home runs. I declined. I explained to him that the only way that I covered my expenses in photographing and producing prints was by the sales thereof. Everyone in the country seemed to love mark McGwire, and certainly Chicago Cubs fans loved Sammy Sosa. Recouping my expenses and making a profit was an easy task regarding those two. However, I had never met anyone who even liked Barry Bonds, much less loved him. The proposal from Michael Barnes was indeed a compliment, but I saw no financial future in the deal. I then went in to Jack Buck's kitchen (through the garage, where he told me that is how his good friends enter) and being somewhat late for our meeting, I told him of the Michael Barnes proposal, and at the time, I think that Barry Bonds was within 5 or so home runs from breaking Mark McGwire's record of 70 home runs. Jack said to me "Do you want Barry Bonds to break McGwire's record?" I said, "Of course not, Jack", he said, "Neither do I, you know for $3,000 we could get Tonya Harding to break his kneecaps!" I said, "Count me in!"

Sometimes my mind wanders and I go off on a different tangent, so getting back to the "What would the World be Without Music" poem that Jack asked me to print for the musicians of the St. Louis Symphony. On Wednesday night I was the guest of Mary Hendin at a "Braggin' Rights" Illinois/Missouri basketball game at the Savvis Center when my phone rang. It was Jack calling, however, for every play on the court there was cheering with an equal number of Mizzou and Illini fans. It was very much like a Cards/Cubs game. The crowd noise was so loud I couldn't hear what he was saying. I said that I would call him back after the game.

I called him back after the game and noticed he had called four more times. Jack answered and asked if I had the symphony prints with me and asked me to come to his house on my way home. I said that I would be there shortly. When I got there, he was wearing his black silk pajamas and looked more frail than I had ever seen him. He said, "I've got cancer, and I am going into the hospital tomorrow morning, and I don't know if I'm coming out, so I wanted to sign these prints for you". Good grief, he was just diagnosed with cancer, yet it was very important for him to follow through on a promise of signing his poems. Not many people would think of that responsibility after receiving such devastating information.

Jack looked at the three prints, signed one for Carole, one for Susan and me, and asked how to sign the one for the orchestra players. I said, "Please sign it "For The Musicians of the St. Louis Symphony Orchestra". Jack said, "I can't do that, I don't know how to spell musicians". I said, "I don't either, let's ask Carole". He said, "No, you don't want to do that, she is sleeping and becomes rather surly when awakened". Anyway, he signed it and thanked me for bringing the prints over at such a late hour. It is hard to imagine anyone but Jack having that incredible sense of responsibility.

Jack Buck had a heart monitor, Parkinson's Disease, was an insulin dependent diabetic, and was just diagnosed with cancer, lung cancer. He told me he was looking forward to getting Alzheimer's Disease because then he would forget he had Parkinson's. Saturday morning after he returned home from his cancer operation that removed 40% from his right lung, called me and said, "Where are you? Come on over, I wrote another poem". The poem was titled "Wake Up" a poem to discourage people from smoking and probably losing lung portions, just like what happened to him. I went over and entered through his garage (and being a good friend that's where I entered) and saw him in his kitchen really looking weak and frail. I said to him, "I hope that all of what you have gone through hasn't affected your sense of humor". He paused a moment, looked at me with those very beady eyes of his, and started slowly maneuvering his right arm and pointed in my direction and said, "UP YOURS!" I said to him, "Jack, I will always cherish that moment."

He said, "Look what they have done to me" and took his shirt off his very skinny torso and revealed the incision on his back where the section of his lung was removed. At the incision there was a fluid sack hanging. He saw that I was looking at it and he said, "I told my doctor about that fluid sack this morning and he asked me how big it was…I told him it was about a 34B". That was Jack, never losing his sense of humor.

MEL FAMIE

I was in Jack Buck's kitchen for another Saturday morning regarding his latest poem and the incorporation of such on one of my photos when he mentioned an incident regarding the pitcher, Mel Famie. I thought I was familiar with most baseball players, both past and present, but I had never heard of Mel Famie. Jack then said that he was a short relief pitcher for the Milwaukee Braves before they moved to Atlanta. Mel Famie was an alcoholic and while in the bullpen, he always brought a very large thermos container that he filled with beer. When he emptied it, Mel would go down the stairs, grab a couple more beers, and reload the thermos. On this particular day during the game between the Chicago Cubs and the Braves, Mel Famie had reloaded his thermos far too many times. The manager called to the bullpen for Mel to warm up so he could come in to pitch the eighth inning. Mel Famie warmed up (it didn't take much as he was already pretty loose) so he could come in.

Jack continued, "So Mel came in and walked the first batter, then the second, then the third, and then the fourth, scoring the eventual winning run. It was discovered after the game that Mel had been totally drunk from so many thermos bottles of beer that the Cubs referred to that beer in the container as 'The beer that made Mel Famie walk us'!"

I was totally roped in and believed Jack until that punch line.

On another occasion with Jack, I was called to assist with the final preparation of several prints that Jack had commissioned as a fund raiser for the Backstoppers, (an organization to help support spouses of fallen firefighters and policemen). It was a print with Mark McGwire's autograph as well as Bob Gibson's, Lou Brock's, Stan Musial's, Red Schoendienst's, and Jack Buck's autographs. Two hundred prints were to be produced to sell for $2,500 each, raising $500,000. David Pratt, part owner of the Cardinals, matched the $500,000, and the print sold out the first day raising $1,000,000 for the Backstoppers. Jack Buck and Lou Brock had to resign three damaged prints. Marty Hendin asked me to be there since our gallery was packaging them and sending them out. We met in the Cooperstown Room at Busch Stadium II for the signing.

Marty Hendin said to Jack, "Jack, you need to thank Don for being here. He should be home packing. He is leaving for Hawaii tomorrow morning."

Jack then looked at me and said, "You are going to Hawaii? While you are there, will you find out if the hula is an ass . . . set to music?"

I asked Jack how long he had been saving that one up. He said this was his first opportunity.

BASEBALL

I was sitting in the Busch Stadium office of my best friend, Marty Hendin, Cardinals vice president, after a baseball game one night when Walt Jocketty, general manager of the Cardinals, opened Marty's door and said that the Memphis Redbirds just won the Pacific Coast League title on a home run by a player name Poo Jols.

Marty and I both said, "Who is that?"

Walt Jocketty said he had just been with the team for three games and didn't know much about him at all.

As I did for many years, I went to spring training with Marty Hendin, and in 2001, I was in the booth with Jack Buck and Mike Shannon when this kid, Poo Jols, was at bat.

I said to Jack, "What about this kid, Pujols? He is hitting around .450 in spring training."

Jack Buck said, "Forget about him. He needs another season or two in the minors, then we will see. He has no experience against Triple-A ball at all."

Maybe so, I thought, but he has faced some pretty good pitchers this spring and handled them very well. Several games later, I was with Marty Hendin in the stands when Albert came to bat again, still hovering around the .400 mark. I said to Marty that this Pujols kid seemed pretty good, could he make the roster up north?

Marty said without any hesitation, "Forget about him. He needs a couple years in the minors."

I was disappointed, but I thought Jack Buck and Marty Hendin certainly knew much more than me. I was just a fan, hungry for offense production, and Albert certainly showed that he was capable of producing many hits and RBIs. Well, as the team was heading north, Bobby Bonilla got hurt and so Albert Pujols came up with the team, never to get his proper seasoning in Memphis. Dagnabbit.

There are several other spring training moments that come immediately to mind. I have loved baseball since I was eight years old. I guess my brother and dad indoctrinated me to the point that I really had no choice but to love it. I think it is the perfect game, so different from all the other major sports. More about that later. At any rate, the point I am making is that I was into my sixties and probably didn't miss many games either in person, on the radio, or on television. That comes close to ten thousand games that I experienced from the time I was eight years old. I thought I knew baseball very well. There was an unoccupied booth on the press level at Roger Dean Stadium in Jupiter, Florida, where I chose to sit and watch one of the spring training games. Marty Hendin and Red Schoendienst came in, sat on either side of me, and started talking about the game. Lucky me, I was sitting with the intelligentsia of baseball flanking me on both sides. Being the watcher of almost ten thousand games, it felt I belonged and was one of the guys.

Red Schoendienst said to Marty, "That kid in left field will never make it."

Marty said, "You are right, never a chance."

What in the hell were they talking about? For all of the games that I had experienced, I never noticed one little nuance, yet a very important little nuance. All of the fielders are kind of moving around, some not, but most of them not very intent on the actions of the pitcher. That is until the pitcher is set at rest before throwing the ball. When the pitcher is set, all of the fielders get set also and lean forward just a little bit on their toes, so to speak, in readiness for the pitch. Red and Marty pointed out that it was almost like a ballet as every fielder gets ready to react to the next pitch. This guy in the left field stood flat-footed and wasn't prepared for the next pitch. I never noticed that one of the more beautiful moments in baseball takes place even before the ball is thrown. I guess I didn't really understand the game.

Back to Red Schoendienst for just a moment. I had gotten to know Red from all of the times I spent in the broadcast booth, just as an observer, due to my friendship with Jack Buck, John Rooney, and Mike Shannon. Several months after my wife of forty-two years, Susan, died, I started seeing a much younger and also very beautiful lady named Marina.

John Rooney and Mike Shannon were talking about my new relationship with this lady to Red, and he came into the booth I was occupying and said, "All right kid, tell me about this new 'very young' lady you are seeing." I showed him her photo on my cell phone. He looked at her, then looked at me, then her again, and said very emphatically, "You're out of your league, kid." I then showed him Susan's photo on my phone. He looked at her, then looked at me, then her again, and said, "You were out of your league then too, kid."

I said, "Gee, thanks, Red. Let's watch the ballgame."

I will speak for a moment to the greatness of the game of baseball as I see it. In every other game, the puck goes into the net, the ball goes through the hoop, the ball crosses the goal line, etc. In baseball, it is the man, not the ball that scores. No score occurs without "the man" crossing the plate. In every other sport, in the last moments of a game, you have the last few minutes to put out a major effort to score. In hockey, for instance, you can get the puck to your best shooter or leave an empty net pulling your goalie and have an extra man on the ice to score. In basketball, you can get the ball to your best three-point scorer. In football, you can pass to your best receiver. In baseball, you can't do that. You just have to wait until the best guy's turn comes up. You just can't insert him at will, so there is so much more strategy in the game. For instance, when Mark McGwire was chasing the home-run record, it seemed like everybody cared about baseball. Those who didn't know how many outs in an inning were hoping that Mark McGwire could come up to bat and hit another home run. This kind of reminded me of the forties in St. Louis. The first question about a game was, "What did Musial do?," and then the next question would be, "Who won?" Simply stated, that was the case with Mark McGwire. What he did was far more important than the game itself. Before any game starts, the lineup is given to the umpires and must be followed throughout the game. In every other major sport, you can take a guy out, give him a rest, then bring him back at will. In football, for God's sake, you even have two separate teams, one for the offense and one for the defense. Not so in baseball. Each player must field his position as well as come to the plate to take his turn at bat. That "at bat" is one of the beauties of baseball. Everyone gets a "one-on-one" with the pitcher. Also, once you take a man out of the game, he is dead meat. You can't put him back in. Also, and probably the greatest difference, there is *no clock*! In the immortal words of Yogi Berra, "It ain't over 'til it's over."

Hotdogs are also better at a baseball game than anywhere else.

Marty Hendin became a friend when I had an idea to photographically depict the breaking of the home-run record of Roger Maris, who broke Babe Ruth's record of sixty home runs by hitting sixty-one in 1960. That record stood for thirty-seven years, much longer than Ruth's record of sixty home runs in 1927. There were only thirty-four years before it was broken. My idea was to crush sixty-two baseballs depicting the breaking of that record, putting them in a pile, and photographing them. I called Marty Hendin, who was the Cardinals vice president in charge of community relations, and told him that I wanted sixty-two baseballs for a photo.

He said, "That is an interesting number, Mr. Marquess. How long will you need them?"

I said, "Mr. Hendin, you won't want them back when I'm through with them."

He said that sounded interesting and he would get back with me. Two days later, I received six dozen brand-new baseballs from Rawlings, the official supplier of baseballs to the major leagues. I was ecstatic. I have almost ruined a four-hundred-dollar suit trying to catch one of those balls at a game and all of a sudden I had seventy-two of them. Marty suggested that as a "thank you," I should give them a print when I completed the photograph. My idea of crushing them went on the back burner as I started to open the boxes. Truly, I was like a kid on Christmas morning. They were gorgeous. It was getting late in the day and the light was warm and wonderful. I drove to a golf course and started to lay them out in a pile, and as I did, I thought these are the "balls of summer." The light was perfect, and my Zeiss 60 macro lens was just the perfect way to capture them on Fuji Velvia film. I was right, the transparencies came back looking just as beautifully as I anticipated. My mind just started racing with ideas for treating the baseball itself as the star of the photos, not a player or a team, just the baseball itself. I went to a fabric store, purchased several yards of different colored silks, and started photographing these gorgeous baseballs. My mind was racing with so many ideas that I couldn't stop. I even went to Molly Brown's fireworks store and purchased several smoke bombs. I picked five of my photos, "The Balls of Summer," "The Patriot," "Old Glory," "Smokin'," and "Pastime," and had the lab make thirty-by-forty-inch Cibachrome prints, framed them, and hung them in my gallery in Plaza Frontenac. The next day, Mark McGwire came in, saw the prints and bought one. The next day, Gary Gaetti, Todd Stottlemeyer, and a couple of other players came in and bought my photos. Marty Hendin called and said that I was creating quite a stir in the Cardinals clubhouse and could he come out and look. I told him that we opened at 9 a.m., but he said that he would be at work by then. Was it possible to open earlier for him, like around 8 a.m.?

I said, "Certainly," and asked my gallery director, Darlene Parks, if she could come in early.

Marty arrived at 8 a.m. and in ten minutes mapped out my next ten years of photographic sales for me.

I was selling my Cibachrome print for $450 each, and he said, "Mr. Marquess, you will soon run out of ball payers that can pop for $450 per print. You need to produce something you can sell for $30 or so." He then said that he would contact the Hall of Fame in Cooperstown, New York. He then said that the Cardinals Hall of

Fame would benefit from having my prints on the walls there. He said that boxes of note cards should be produced and would sell well.

All that in ten minutes or so. Marty Hendin had the greatest promotional mind that I had ever experienced.

When he left, Darlene, the gallery director, was in tears, saying, "Oh Don, this is it. He loves it."

Marty and I became close friends and shared lunch at least once a week for over ten years.

At that point, my original idea of crushing sixty-two baseballs was placed on the back burner.

An Unforgettable
Evening at Busch Stadium

I was at a gas station filling my tank when Susan called on my cell phone. This was September 16, 1997 early in the afternoon, and she said that at 2 p.m., there was to be an important announcement from the Cardinals in a press conference. I immediately turned to KMOX to hear Bill DeWitt announce the signing of Mark McGwire to a three-year contract. *Incredible*! Mark McGwire was traded to the Cardinals at the July 31 deadline, and many St. Louis fans assumed that he was just a "rent-a-player" and at the end of the year, he would opt for free agency and sign for the top dollar in MLB. This announcement was indeed one of the more pleasant surprises in my forty-five-plus years of Cardinals mania.

Then Mark McGwire took the podium and said many things that I wanted to hear from players for years.

He said, "First of all, I love St. Louis and the Cardinals fans. Many friends told me that I would love playing here, and they were absolutely right. I love coming to the stadium each day to play the game I love, and I'm in front of packed houses for every game at Busch Stadium." What a perfect opening statement. Then he said, "Many of my player friends thought that I should go to free agency and go to the highest bidder. Well, let me tell you, I know a lot of guys that did that, and they aren't very happy. I can tell you now, I am *very* happy here. It blows my mind how much money we players are paid to play this game. My new contract is worth a lot of money, and I am very happy with that amount. How much money does anyone need anyway?" (His contract was for three years and $28.5 million dollars. He was right, that is a lot of money.) Next, he said, "I am also donating one million per year for sexually and physically abused children." Another good deed! Mark McGwire said everything that an appreciative and honorable gentleman would say, and I loved it.

I called Susan to see if she wanted to go to the game that night, and she said, "Definitely."

I had given away our season tickets for that game, but we planned on buying a couple of tickets from a scalper on the street that evening. We couldn't wait for the game as we were so excited. We bought the tickets and got into the stadium. The usher in our section knew us well enough and found a couple of empty seats close to our season seats. We looked around and saw several people that had season seats close to ours sitting in different seats than usual. We were not the only ones that came to the game due to Mark McGwire's press conference. This was a meaningless game late in September when both the Dodgers and the Cardinals were out of contention for postseason play. Under normal conditions, such a meaningless game (if there really could be a meaningless Cardinals game) would have maybe fourteen thousand fans or so. There must have been close to thirty thousand people in the stands!

Mark McGwire was the third to bat in the first inning. He came up to the plate, and thirty thousand fans stood and cheered. Usually when that happens, after the first pitch, everyone sits down . . . not so this time. Fans stood and cheered through the first four pitches, and on the fifth pitch that Ramon Martinez threw, Mark McGwire hit the longest home run ever hit in Busch Stadium that traveled 517 feet to left center field and dotted the "I" in his name on the batter's sign. (He later eclipsed that by hitting one to dead center field 545 feet, which may be the longest home run ever recorded in MLB.)

People were high fiveing people next to them and everyone had watery eyes! What an unforgettable night at Busch. The Cardinals lost to the Dodgers 7–6, but no matter.

John Rooney, The Pro

Through my friend, Marty Hendin, I met John Rooney, the newly hired broadcaster for the Cardinals in 2006 who was stolen from the White Sox after fourteen years or so as their broadcaster. John is the only baseball announcer to broadcast World Series winners back-to-back for two different teams: the Chicago White Sox in 2005 and the St. Louis Cardinals in 2006. John and I met on a Cardinals Cruise and became immediate friends. John has a quick and unfailing wit and keeps me laughing. He invited me for five spring trainings to stay with him in his rented condo in Jupiter. After each trip, my sides ached for several days from laughing so hard. If baseball ever comes to an end, John could make a great living doing voice-overs for Saturday morning cartoons. John has a terrific ear for voices and does a Harry Caray better than Harry himself, a wonderful Vin Scully, Tom Brokaw, Pat Buttram, and countless others.

I asked John why he didn't use those voices on the broadcasts, and he said, "Because it is about the game, not about me!"

I will never forget that he said that and that he meant it. Fans are hearing exactly what is happening in the game as described excellently by John Rooney, but they have no inkling of his wit and ability to entertain with the many voices he possesses. Truly, John Rooney is the consummate professional.

One morning in Jupiter for spring training, there was a day off with no game, and John was sleeping in. He was going to wake up around 10 a.m. and we were going to have a fun day in beautiful sunny Southern Florida. We were going to stop at the ballpark (Roger Dean Stadium), then head down to Ft Lauderdale to the Seminole Hard Rock Casino to play a little blackjack, then head to his favorite restaurant for the best pasta fagioli soup on the planet. It was to be a great day!

Not so . . . the lawn guys started mowing and trimming the condo lawn at 7 a.m., waking John and depriving him of three more hours of desired slumber. He tossed and turned for an hour or so, finally gave up, and came out of his room. Then we headed for the ballpark about twenty or so miles away. We got about two miles from the park when John realized that he had forgotten what he needed to take to it, so we turned around and headed back to the condo. John has a terrific sense of humor; however, it was not very apparent at this time. On the way back to the condo, John wanted to stop at Starbucks for a cappuccino and a scone. The store was packed and the drive up was six cars deep, and then it started raining. We finally got the breakfast items, made it back to the condo, John got his stuff, we dropped it off at the stadium, and headed for Fort Lauderdale. The traffic was horrible, all the construction was in full swing, the rain was now a deluge, and things were generally stinky. Finally, we made it to the Hard Rock, parked the car, and walked in looking for the blackjack tables. No luck! No blackjack at the Hard Rock. They gave some flimsy excuse for no tables, but it didn't make us feel any better. We played slots and a little roulette until it came time for dinner. John lost in slots (big surprise), but John said that we were just about fifteen minutes away from this great restaurant with the fabulous pasta fagioli soup, so everything would be great. The rain stopped and the temperature was around ninety humid degrees and completely overcast. We headed for the restaurant, and when we got there, it was closed! Monday, it was closed. John was ruined. I said to John that a restaurant Tony La Russa liked named Nick's Tomato Pie had a great pasta fagioli soup, and if he could wait, so could I. It was about seventy-five miles away and about ten miles north of Jupiter, but why not, we both could wait. The journey back was worse than the trip down, and all the drivers were idiots. John, on several occasions, yelled at the idiot driver ahead of us and other times just yelled at no one in particular. It started raining again, this time like a monsoon.

We finally made it to Nick's Tomato Pie, and the lot was packed. John asked me to get out and get a table, and he would park the car and come in. There was one table left, so I procured it immediately and asked for the waitress.

She arrived, and I said to her, "There is a man coming in to join me. He is going to ask for pasta fagioli soup, and you are going to tell him that you are out of that soup. Please do that."

She said she would, and as we looked up, a soaking wet John Rooney was headed for our table. John was exhausted, crabby, and wet.

He asked for pasta fagioli soup, and she said, "Sorry, sir, we are out of that soup."

John exploded and said that he was going to the drive-through at *McDonald's. She immediately laid the blame on me and told him that they had plenty.*

John looked at me and said, "I am not going to the drive-through at McDonald's, and you can walk home."

Then he laughed, although I don't think he enjoyed that little prank as much as I did.

THE HONEYMOON
(ALMOST)

In 1968, Susan and I were married on September 20. We took a major trip together that previous summer. I was planning a trip to Phoenix to see a friend and then stop in Las Vegas. Susan wanted to visit her sister in San Francisco and would ride with me to Las Vegas, where then she would catch a bus to San Francisco. However, it was great that after several days on the road, her sister's visit was no longer a goal. To use Susan's own words, we were "goofy in love" and just decided to complete wherever I was headed to head there together.

On my favorite driving trip across the Great Southwest through Oklahoma and the Texas Panhandle, there's a stop at the Big Texan restaurant where its free seventy-two-ounce steak is served. It's free only if you can finish it along with a salad, shrimp cocktail, and baked potato in an hour. If you *don't* finish it, the cost was, as I remember, $42. Somewhat hefty, even for 1968. We stopped and had two small steaks, which neither one of us finished.

New Mexico was beautiful as always, where the stars at night are big and bright, deep in the heart of New Mexico. I know it doesn't have the same poetic flow as deep in the heart of Texas, but I defy anyone to find a larger cluster of brightly twinkling stars anywhere on this planet than in New Mexico. We continued my favorite trip (especially now with Susan as my companion) and turned north at Flagstaff and reached the south rim of LeGrande Canyon. Susan had never seen it, and as I looked at it once again with Susan standing on the edge, it was never more beautiful. We stayed the night at the El Tovar Lodge, saw the sunrise over the canyon, and then headed south toward Phoenix to visit an old "Group" friend, Ronnie Thoene, where we would play an assassins game of Monopoly. Of course, I wiped everybody out. I tried to talk Ronnie into meeting us in Las Vegas, but he declined. We then drove north to old Route 66, then west to Kingman, Arizona (the home of Andy Devine), and turned right to head north to Las Vegas . . . maybe my favorite place on earth.

We arrived in Las Vegas, and the Castaways called to me. The Castaways casino was eventually torn down for the building of the Mirage with its fiery water spewing from the man-made volcano. The Castaways had a Polynesian theme, and it was just a storybook location. I was there with the most beautiful lady in the world and was very ready to win some "big bucks." I was well prepared as I had $200 in my wallet and had hidden another $200 in my suitcase that I didn't tell me about. You know, just in case things turned very sour. Around 8 p.m. or so, I approached a $3 table and started working on my fortune. I took $50 from my wallet and bought in. Beautiful Susan, in her white lace dress with a touch of turquoise piping around the neck and sleeves, stood behind me and watched. I was very lucky getting cards and betting them properly. Betting $3 a hand eventually caused my "buy-in stake" to reach $100. During the evening, I never went back in my pocket for another $50. Susan was very impressed, which really set the tone for our next forty-two years together and her very positive belief in my blackjack playing. Susan didn't gamble at all, so she walked around the casino a lot.

Around 10:30 p.m. or so, she stopped back at the table and said, "Don, I'm really sleepy. I'm going to the room. Wake me up when you come to bed."

The dealer looked at me as if I were a fool to turn down such an invitation, but I continued playing anyway. This also set a precedent for many years to come. If I turned down her invitation in Las Vegas, she knew I couldn't be tempted to leave the table by those Vegas bimbos.

Night went on and on, and in the morning I was still at the same table (a definite no-no from inveterate gamblers) when Susan tapped me on the shoulder and said, "Good morning, sailor, how are you?"

I had been extraordinarily lucky and had built up quite a stake. I still had not gone back in my pocket for another $50. She was standing behind me when I was dealt a pair of sevens to the dealer's six showing. My wagers had grown to $20 per hand, so I split and put up another $20. The first seven was hit with a four, so I doubled down on that and put up another $20. Now I have $60 on one hand of blackjack. The next seven was hit with another seven, so I split again . . . there goes another $20. The first seven was hit with a three, so I doubled down with another $20. At this point, I was trying desperately to remain very calm and professional; however, my right leg started vibrating. The next seven (four total) was hit with a ten, so I stayed. The dealer flipped his cards, and just as I hoped, he had a ten in the hole. Sixteen total, he had to hit. It was another seven! *Bust*! I won $120 on that one hand, however complex, of blackjack. Susan was so impressed that I felt that cloud nine had just passed by and we hopped on. I won over $1,300 with that evening's play. The pit boss came over and offered to buy breakfast for us. After breakfast, we went to check out of our room and pay the bill.

The hotel desk clerk said, "No charge, sir. The Castaways has paid for your room."

That one evening cemented my love for Las Vegas that continues to this day.

We then loaded the car with our luggage and my winnings and headed toward the Mexican border. Susan spoke fluent Spanish. I had three years of Latin, but very few people spoke conversational Latin, so I was relying totally on her as my interpreter. We crossed the border just south of Tucson and entered through Nogales. What seemed like a thundering hoard of eight-year-old Mexican waifs surrounded me upon arriving in Nogales, asking for money to watch my car. I became very nervous, but Susan came to my rescue and said something to those kids, and they skedaddled.

I learned several very important phrases such as "Dos Pepsis, por favor," "Donde esta el banyo?," as well as my breakfast order, "Buenos dias, senorita. Quisiero tener daysauna? Dos huevos con jamon e café negro, por favor." Every time I visited Mexico since, those simple phrases came in very handily.

We continued due south to Hermosillo, a thriving (?) town in northern Sonoma. It appeared to be around 110 degrees but felt like 180 or so, so we stopped at the first hotel/motel that had a swimming pool and checked in immediately. We had a great time in the pool as long as we were submerged. Afterwards, we went to our room, changed for dinner, and entered the restaurant, which had a band playing. There were maybe fifty or so people at tables, and when we walked in, the bandleader tapped his baton on the podium. The band stopped playing, then the band started playing a different song. Everyone stood and applauded toward us. To this day, I don't know for sure who they thought we were, but I have speculated with many possibilities. Susan closely resembled Cher, Barbara Feldon (99 in *Get Smart*), and Marlo Thomas. She also bore a strong resemblance to Jane Fonda. It is possible that the hotel could have mistaken her for a celebrity. Another thought that occurred to me was, perhaps it was my name that confused them. Marquess is a British title, just below a duke, so maybe that confused them. We were happy with the standing ovation anyway.

After a luscious dinner with pineapple pie for dessert, we made it back to the room. We entered the room, and the temperature and humidity were just like outside. Steamy! We put on our pajamas and soon realized that sleep was impossible. It was unbearably hot and humid.

I called the front desk and the clerk kept saying, "Mucho color, mucho color."

Susan helped by saying we wanted mucho frio. He didn't seem to care. So just dressed in our pajamas and morning clothes, we left that hotel with our luggage and drove to a nearby hotel/motel that had neon icicles flashing on and off. Before signing the book, we had asked to enter the room . . . it was ice-cold. *Bingo*!

We had a beautiful evening sleep in the air-conditioned room. We found out later that "air-cooled" from the first motel basically meant a fan blowing over a pan of water. The next morning, upon awakening, Susan had heard many great things about Guymos, a vacation village directly on the Sea of Cortez that was due south of Hermosillo, and she thought it would make a nice day trip. So, without checking out of the second hotel (we had also not checked out of the first hotel), we headed for Guymos. We like it so much that we checked into a resort to spend the night.

This was a night that we paid for three hotel rooms in Mexico, and as I recall, the total amount of all three hotels was $34. *Total*! Our premarriage honeymoon could not have been any better.

What a magnificent trip.

Burt Reynolds ~ Peachtree Plaza

It was early in 1981 when the Ceramic Tile Distributors Convention was held at the Peachtree Plaza Hotel in Atlanta. While I was standing in line checking in at the hotel, my good friend, Bill Haslett, the district manager for a German tile manufacturer, saw me in line and came up to speak with me. The usual "How are you, what's new, etc." were exchanged, and then the really important subject of where we would dine that evening was discussed. There was a sign next to the registration desk advertising Nikolai's Restaurant, which boasted five stars and wonderful French/Russian cuisine. Bill and I both thought that sounded just fine for dinner that evening, and so we asked about a reservation. The lady at the desk said that they were booked five months in advance and dinner for us that evening was a pipe dream, so we decided to look elsewhere. Other acquaintances saw us and started conversing, so we tabled our dinner venue discussions.

Later that afternoon, the owner of Epro Tile, Suzi Stillson, a tile manufacturer that I represented in St. Louis, called and invited me to dinner that evening at Nikolai's. Stupefied, I asked how she managed to get the reservation when they were booked five months in advance. She said that she called a friend in Pittsburgh who made the reservation. Not asking any further questions about that, I asked if I could bring my friend, Bill Haslett. She said, of course, she knew

Bill and he was always a welcome guest. She had a table for six and there was room for Bill. It was dinner at 7:30 p.m., and Bill and I were pleasantly surprised and definitely up for it.

Nikolai's Restaurant was an elite white tablecloth and tuxedoed waiter's restaurant and one of the most elegant dining rooms I had experienced. The host escorted all six of us to the table, and the table next to us was occupied by Burt Reynolds, Brian Keith, and a few others. They were there for the filming of *Sharky's Machine*. All six of us were greatly impressed. I can't remember who the other three guests at our table were, nor who the other three or four at Burt Reynolds' table. I feel certain that if one of them was either Sally Field or Loni Anderson, I would remember, so apparently neither was at the table.

The entire event, dining at a restaurant that had a five-month wait, and a table next to Burt Reynolds put all of us in a very giddy mood. It was an evening where everything was funny, and we laughed at just about anything continuously until the waiter came to take our orders. The waiter informed us that a specialty of the house for dessert was their Grand Marnier soufflé. And since it would take a long time to prepare, we needed to order it when we ordered our meals. That sounded just great to all of us, so we ordered three soufflés. I remember clearly that I ordered an entrée of a venison stew, which was delicious. My chair was to the back of the Burt Reynolds table, so I couldn't see him during dinner. Everybody else could, though, and it was hard to make eye contact with the other diners at our table. Everything that was said at our table caused a giddy response from us, and I began to think we were making a scene. The dining highlight, the Grand Marnier soufflé, was being placed directly in front of Bill and I. The waiter then scooped a long cylinder of frozen whipped cream and laid it on the center of the oblong soufflé bowl. As the steaming soufflé began to melt the frozen cream, the cylinder started to turn vertical and sink. Saying nothing, I saluted as if it were a sinking ship. Bill noticed this first and broke up in laughter. Everyone else at the table also saw me saluting and laughed uproariously. We were definitely making a scene and somewhat out of place in this very elegant room.

After the check came, which was paid by Suzi (great news), we all got up to leave. I turned to the table of Burt Reynolds, who was wearing a tan corduroy jacket with blue jeans, and said to him, "I know this has been driving you crazy all evening, but I *am* Don Marquess!" He exploded with laughter as did the rest of his table.

KAREN – BUSCH STADIUM ATTENDANT

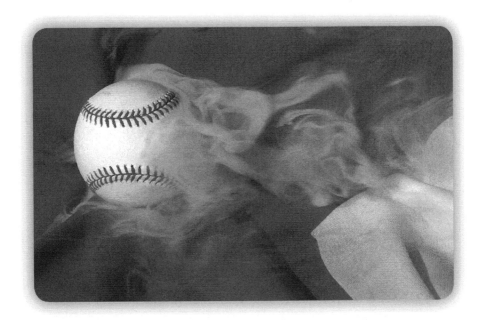

My brother and his wife, Millie, didn't visit very often since they lived about five hundred miles away in Shreveport, Louisiana. But when they did visit, it was always an enjoyable meeting. At the end of one particular visit, we were all in my driveway saying "goodbye," "have a safe trip home," etc., when Millie asked Susan about Natalie, Susan's sister in Sonoma, California. Sadly, that answer was not a short one. After about ten minutes of Natalie talk, Susan made the blunder of asking Millie about one of her thirteen brothers and sisters. Millie talked for about eleven minutes (she just had to outdo Susan) talking about her sisters Linda and Ann. Okay, that should have been it . . . "Goodbye, have a great trip home." But no, Susan asked Millie about Bruce and Steve, her sons. Egad, that went on for another fifteen minutes or so. I was getting very restless because now it was 12:30 p.m. and the Cardinals game was starting at 1:15 p.m. I lived and died with my beloved Cardinals (One year, I attended seventy-five of their eighty-one home games), and our house was about twenty minutes from the stadium. So, say goodbye again for God's sake and make it take this time! No luck. More questions and very lengthy answers. Finally, after about fifteen minutes, they got in the car and backed out of our driveway. I kissed and hugged beautiful Susan, and got in my car thirty minutes before the first pitch to the visiting Los Angeles Dodgers. Hoping there were no radar police vehicles on I-44, I raced to the ballpark.

I always parked at the same lot directly across the street from Busch, and Karen, the parking lot attendant, always placed an orange cone in my parking spot. I made the mistake of tipping her $20 the first game of the year (opening day) and I became her lifetime friend, and she always had that cone in my spot. The game was starting in eight minutes when I arrived. She moved the cone, and I parked in my spot right next to the street, so all I would have to do is park, exit, and trot across the street to the entrance just around the stadium to my entrance gate and I wouldn't miss the first pitch. Not today. Karen heard Jack Buck mention my name on the Cardinals broadcast regarding one of my photographs during the game before on Saturday and she wanted to talk about it. Good grief, doesn't anyone understand the importance of the first pitch? Well, I had to be polite and chat a little. I didn't want to be rude to the lady that held my spot on the lot, so I chatted for a few minutes before I got out of the car into the ninety-plus-degree weather to get to the game. I almost ran into the entrance, stopped at my favorite refreshment counter, purchased my jumbo dog with mustard, relish, and jalapenos, my bag of peanuts, my large Diet Coke, and just made it to my seat in time for the first pitch. Whew, I actually made it despite all of the chattery delays. However, when I reached in my pocket for my money clip, I didn't feel my car keys. Maybe I put them in my other pocket. No time to think about that now, the game was starting. I took one big bite of my dog, slurped on my Diet Coke, and opened my scorecard for a glorious day of baseball. Clear blue skies, slight balmy breezes, and a ninety-plus-degree temperature, I would get my keys out of my other pocket at the end of the game. This game was tied in the bottom of the ninth 3–3 and went into extra innings. The game ended with the Cardinals beating the "Dodgahs" 5–3 in the bottom of the twelfth inning. A usual, two-and-a-quarter-hour game was pushing four hours, but I was very happy (baseball games can't last too long for me, especially with a Cardinals victory), so I started to head for the parking lot to fetch my new Lexus (only three months old).

I exited the stadium and reached in my right pocket for my keys. Oh, oh, no keys. I searched my left pocket once again . . . no keys. My other pockets had the same result. Now, as I was about to round the stadium, I thought I may have dropped them outside of the car. Oh boy, a new Lexus with keys on the concrete parking lot floor just inviting someone to take my car and drive it away. I thought my car would be gone. However, as I rounded the stadium, I saw my car standing alone in my perfect parking spot. It was the only car left on the lot as many people left early due to the extra inning game. As I got to my car, I started looking around the front door of the car hoping I would see the keys . . . No luck, no keys! I thought maybe they dropped on the floor of the car, so I hoped I hadn't locked it. I reached the door handle, opened the door, . . . and . . . a . . . freezing blast of cold air hit me in the face! I had left the car running for almost four hours right in front of Busch Stadium where forty thousand-plus fans saw the game. Probably ten thousand people or more walked past my car.

That says many things. The engine of my Lexus was super quiet, and Cardinals fans are honest upstanding citizens (who apparently didn't hear the engine running).

WHAT TIME IS IT?

When I was seventeen, I started my first year at Missouri University. I had never been away to live before, and my mom's baby (me) was leaving home. She was very worried that I would oversleep and miss my morning classes, so she bought an alarm clock for me. This was no ordinary alarm clock, although it looked like many I had seen before, with a planger of some sort resting between two round-shaped bells. The bells could cause severe hearing loss if you didn't turn it off in time. However, that was not what made it so horribly treacherous. It didn't just ticktock, it *TICKTOCKED!* The sound was deafening. My roommate, Roger, thought it was the most obnoxious sound he had ever heard. Finally, after trying many parts of our dorm room that would somewhat soften the unrelenting *tick tock, tick tock*, we decided to put it in the closet with the door closed tightly. Still, with the lights out and in our respective beds, we could still hear, just like Poe's Pendulum . . . *tick tock tick tock tick tock*!

I need to tell you that our dorm was brand-spanking-new and was just constructed in the middle of a field on the campus. There were four structures that were basically monuments to mediocrity, just simple concrete block structures with the distinct and very imaginative names of C, D, E, and F. We were in Hall F. (Apparently, someone named Hyde had made a donation of some sort, so our half of the building was named Hyde House in Hall F.) Our building was just a cow pasture away from Crowder Hall, the feeding trough for freshmen.

One morning at breakfast, the occupants of the room directly below us were talking about the obnoxious noises they were hearing from the field as they were trying to go to sleep at night . . . cows mooing, dogs barking, and probably a few mountain lions roaring. Hyde House, Hall F had no air-conditioning, so all of the room windows were kept open. My roommate and I never heard these feral sounds, as they were all shielded from our ears by the incessant *ticktocking* of the monster clock.

Later that evening as nighty-night time had arrived and while listening to the killer clock's never-ending *tick tock tick tock*, I said to my roommate, Roger, "With all of the weird sounds our dorm mates are hearing, what would they think of hearing our (my) clock outside their window?" I was thinking that it would really make them wonder what would come next. We rigged up a sling of sorts with two belts, attached the killer clock, and slowly started lowering it to what we felt would be their window. The ticking was deafening. We held tight to our suspending strap waiting to hear them being awakened by yet another strange sound when suddenly, the sling went limp. I knew that our makeshift strapping had given away and the monster clock had fallen to its death in a crashing blow to the ground beneath. I, while in my pajamas, left the room, went down the stairs, and around the back of Hall F. I had no flashlight and it was a cloudy night, so I had no assistance of moonlight. My roommate, Roger, was at our window waiting to hear the damage report. He called to me asking if I had found it, and I said, "No, dang it," thinking it must have bounced somewhere close to the building.

Our neighbors, the victims of our caper, apparently were awakened by my roommate and me talking about the loss, and one of them called through their window and asked, "What are you doing outside waking us up when it is so late?"

I said, "I lost something and can't find it."

They said, "What did you lose?"

I said, "My alarm clock."

They said, "Your alarm clock? How could you lose an alarm clock outside of the building?"

I replied, "That's a story for another time, but in the meantime, where in the hell did it land? I think I should be able to find a piece of it or something."

"How can you lose an alarm clock? Wait until morning, then you will find it," they both said.

My roommate, Roger, just said, "Come back. I'll help you when it is light in the morning."

So I went back upstairs, turned out the light, and got into bed . . . still worried about my alarm clock. Then I heard . . . *tick tock* . . . tick tock . . . *tick tock* coming from under my bed. It was the *killer clock*!

Then my roommate and the downstairs neighbors, who were hiding outside our door, started laughing uproariously. The ticking of the clock did indeed awaken them, and they looked out their window and saw my clock dangling. They retrieved it and just let me search for it. A big *haha*!

THE MOST INCREDIBLE DAY

We, the Missouri Brick Company, were supplying a new slip-resistant floor tile to a facility in Branson, Missouri, named White Water, a fantastic water park the likes of which neither of us, Bill Haslett nor I, had ever seen. Bill Haslett was the U.S. representative for the German manufacturer of the tile we furnished for that water park. White Water was around 250 miles away, so we left around 5:30 in the morning for our 10 a.m. meeting. The tile was a brand-new product manufactured in Giessen, West Germany, named "Grip Glaze." It had a very high coefficient of friction and was pure white resembling a slightly puffy cotton ball. Just an explanation regarding "coefficient of friction," that meant that bare feet, leather, and rubber would not slide nor slip easily on its surface. The only problem with it was White Water was having a difficult time cleaning it, and the mops they were using were leaving fabric traces on the floor. Bill and I went to a hardware store and purchased a proper sponge mop and the problem was solved. We felt very heroic and we left them very happy.

When we left around dawn to travel to Branson, Missouri, we had four hours or so of conversation, which was great because we were good friends and enjoyed each other's company. After our meeting in Branson, we decided that if we had time, we would stop in Union, Missouri (sort of on the way back), and meet with a fabricator on a sizable federal project. Our discussions also included big fun because later there was to be a Cardinals/Cubs game at Busch Stadium in St.

Louis and maybe we could make it back in time for that. Also, Bill Haslett was a big fan of horse racing, and just across the Mississippi from St. Louis was Fairmont Park, the local horse racetrack. Wow, what grandiose plans for one day. I also told Bill that if we had time to make it to the racetrack, I would bet the trifecta, and if I won, I would give him 10% of my winnings.

Well, well, everything worked out perfectly, all visits turned out positively, and all of our meetings were very productive, and they were over soon enough to give us enough time to pick up my son, Donny, and make it to Busch just before the first pitch. The game was over quickly (Cards won and beat those stinking Cubs), so we had enough time to make it to Fairmont Park for the last couple of races. I picked a horse in the eighth race that won and paid $4.80. So for my $10 wager, I won $24. The next race was better. I picked the winner and won the exacta and my win wager . . *ka-ching*, and another $182.75. Things were going very well. Then the tenth race with the trifecta race was coming up. I placed my usual bet of $6 on the trifecta, $10 on the exacta, and $10 to win. My evening was going very well. The long shot I picked as the third horse finished first, so sadly, I lost my win bet and my exacta bet. However the trifecta paid $1,850. What an incredible day. When we walked out to pick up my car from the valet, it was already waiting for us.

I counted out $185 to give to Bill for his promised percentage, and he received it very graciously . . . at least for a little while.

Then he said, "You know, I am really mad. This morning on our way to Branson, you knew you were going to win the trifecta. You knew! If you didn't know you were going to win, you would have given me half instead of this lousy $185!"

What an incredible day.

Trip to Shreveport

As mentioned previously, Susan would not get on an airplane for any reason, so our travels together were always auto or train. I had planned to visit my brother in Shreveport, and Susan thought that a train trip would be just swell. I have no aversion to train travel. As a matter of fact, all of my trips to Europe have been with Eurail Pass—the only way to travel in Europe. Amtrak rail travel is significantly different in the USA. They use the same tracks as the freight trains (which gives great stress to the tracks, so the ride is not quite as smooth as the European trains). Also in the Midwest, freight rules, so the passenger trains do not receive the same priority.

Nevertheless, I was game for our train adventure to Shreveport. However, at that time there was no direct travel from St. Louis to Shreveport, so my brother would have to pick us up in Texarkana, Arkansas, and we would be traveling on the train for over fourteen hours. What a wonderful time for togetherness . . . hmm. Train travel in Europe consists of individual compartments that seat two or three on each side facing each other. My experience traveling during the day was that most compartments were empty and stretching out was great in the empty compartment. Not so in the USA. The train cars were more like bus or airplane seats. Susan and I went to the last section of the rail car where two seats were facing each other. These seats were available only at either end of the car.

When Susan was in college, she worked during the summer at a bank in Woodbury, New Jersey. She did this for several summers and really enjoyed it. The Bank of Woodbury (I think) was also a bank that offered employment to handicapped high school and college students during the Ssmmer recess. One of the students was hearing-challenged and used sign language. This student taught Susan the sign language alphabet, which Susan then taught me. Herein the story develops.

It had gotten late and many of the passengers in our car, I assumed, were sleeping, or at least trying to, so I didn't want to disturb them with my booming voice. I got Susan's attention and signed "Hi."

She picked up on that and signed "Hi" back to me.

I then signed, "What is cooking, babe?" (I should point out that my expertise in signing was not with continuous and fluid motions. I had to think about each letter and form them, so she could understand, but being the fast learner, I thought I was becoming better with each word.)

Susan said to me with those beautiful hands of hers: "Hey, sailor, what are you doing later tonight?" She was warming up to this whole idea.

Then I said, "Did you hear about the traveling salesman who stopped at a farmhouse?" I was getting more and more dramatic with my hand motions and was actually creating a stir in the rail car with the other passengers. I couldn't see this because I was facing Susan, who was in the last seat in the car. She started laughing. This encouraged me to continue (showbiz), you know. Then I, very dramatically, started to sing to her with my hand signals (I was on a roll): "Old man ribber, that old man ribber . . .," Getting more animated with each line. Susan lost control and started laughing really, really hard. I was still not realizing that I had caused a curiosity with the rest of the car, and everyone was watching my wild gesticulations.

Just then, a man across the aisle reached over, tapped me on the shoulder, and spoke very loudly and distinctly, pronouncing every word, saying, "*What . . . time . . . is . . . it?*"

This was my moment of truth. I had to make a decision, one way or the other. I said nothing but reached my hand across the aisle and showed him my watch. I had done it. I made a commitment to be deaf and able to speak in sign language only for the rest of our trip. I just couldn't let the man know, so I had to remain speechless. Susan, who had a remarkable sense of humor, realized the situation in which I had placed myself, gained her composure, and accepted the fact that I had to be totally nonverbal. From that point on, we could only converse in sign language. After several hours, we left that car and went to the next car.

As soon as the door closed, we both said, *"Let's talk!"*

Ducks on Parade

My brother lived and practiced in Shreveport, Louisiana, and he was also my CPA, a damn good one I might add. I had a lot of "splainin'" to do with my income and expenditures, so it seemed like a trip to visit him was in order. This was in the spring as the Cardinals were heading north for the regular season. They were making stops in Louisville (Redbirds) and Memphis (Chicks) along their trip to St. Louis. My plan was to see both games on our way to Shreveport. They were playing a game in Memphis, which was the home of the very famous Peabody Hotel. It was the first trip in a while for the two of us, and I made a reservation for us on an executive (very exclusive as well as very expensive) floor. The Peabody Hotel is well known for a very unusual tradition of marching ducks. I told Susan about this phenomenon, and she couldn't wait to see it. I had stayed at the Peabody Hotel in Orlando, Florida, where the same tradition continued. Every morning at around 11 a.m. or so, the elevator opens on the lobby floor and a man wearing a top hat and a tuxedo with tails, and who is holding a long baton, not unlike a drum major at a college football game, emerges followed by a dozen or so ducks. These beautiful, brown, multicolored, and highly disciplined English call ducks march in line to the *King Cotton* march and jump into the fountain lobby pool. They stay and frolic in the pool all day until five o'clock or so until the elevator opens again and the same tuxedoed and top-hatted leader comes to the pond, the marching music starts again and the ducks jump out of the pool and march in line to the elevator. It is truly a wonder to behold. They must be very smart ducks.

Susan was really looking forward to seeing it. There is a coffee shop/restaurant very close to where the ducks do their marching, so we decided to go down early and have a pre-"duck watch" snack. I had been very busy with my work, so Susan and I didn't have many opportunities to just sit and talk. She was telling a story about what I don't remember, but I was enraptured. The Peabody has been in existence since 1869 and probably the dishes and glassware that were used at the restaurant were the originals from that time. The reason I am mentioning this is that their glasses are not just glasses—they are very heavy sculpted red glasses. I am an ice chewer, and after drinking water, the ice cubes are a delicacy for an ice chewer. After chewing several cubes, that last one must be swirled and loosened so the last cube can slip down and be consumed. Well, as Susan was still finishing her story, unknown to me, the waitress had filled my glass again with water. I turned to get that last ice morsel, not noticing the difference in weight, swirled the glass, and threw the entire glass of water in my face. It was an absolutely ridiculous thing to do. I was dumbstruck, and Susan was astonished and laughing hysterically. I looked around and half the restaurant was looking at me and laughing. I was blank-faced. Now, further unfortunately, I was wearing khakis, and with the water explosion, my pants looked like I had a major bladder accident. I could not get up and reveal the huge wet area of my pants, but duck time was fast approaching. We sat, hoping my pants would dry somewhat and I could walk to the lobby. I loaded my lap with towels that the laughing waitress delivered trying to speed-dry my pants, but it still looked ridiculous. Then we heard the ducks' marching music.

Susan said, "I don't care how you look, we are going to see those damn ducks. Follow me."

So like two dogs doing the nasty, I walked behind Susan, and with the march blaring, we made it to the lobby. Unfortunately, the crowd was about five deep and all we saw was the ring master's top hat as the elevator door was closing. We had a very silent road trip from Memphis to Shreveport.

THE CRUSHING OF THE BALLS

In 1998, there were several possibilities of players who had the ability to beat Roger Maris's record of sixty-one home runs in a single season. Andres Gallaraga who hit forty-one home runs for the Rockies in 1997, Ken Griffey Jr. who hit fifty-six for the Mariners the year before, and our player, Mark McGwire, who hit a total of fifty-eight in 1997 between the Oakland A's and the St. Louis Cardinals, and Sammy Sosa who hit thirty-six with the stinkin' Cubs in 1997. My hopes were on McGwire to break the sixty-one home-run record.

My grandfather started a machine company in 1917 and had many types of machines that I felt were capable of assisting me in achieving my goal depicting the breaking of the record. I contacted my uncle, Virgil, and told him what I wanted to achieve—the crushing of one side of the baseballs as if they had been struck on one side by a baseball bat. My uncle then had a stainless-steel mold made by some company in Tennessee that the ball could rest in as well as a stainless-steel rod that has the diameter of the sweet spot on a bat. They had a thirty-thousand-pound hydraulic press and fitted it with the ball support and the "bat." I brought the sixty-two balls to his company, Multiple Boring Machine Company, and the process commenced. I stood by, cutting the seams of some so it would appear that they were hit so hard that the seams split.

The balls looked like they had truly been hit by a bat, and I had achieved my goal.

That year, 1998, Mark McGwire didn't just beat the record of sixty-one home runs, but he crushed it, hitting seventy home runs. I took just one of the crushed balls and two uncrushed balls and put them in a simple composition titled *The Babe, Roger, and Mark*, with Mark McGwire's the only one in color and the rest of the balls in the photo are in sepia. We sold out in two weeks.

My original idea of just showing sixty-two crushed baseballs was put on hold once again.

DARLENE THEUSCH
(NÉE GARDNER)

I opened my gallery in Plaza Frontenac Mall in 1995. Due to the hours required by the mall owners, I needed it to be open seventy-two hours per week. My son, Daniel, covered forty of those hours, but additional help was needed. Lucky for me, a recent art and photography major from Southwest Missouri State stopped by and applied for a job. She was hired immediately due to the fact that she was knowledgeable about art, quite personable, and very attractive. Darlene had all of the necessary attributes to promote and handle sales at the gallery. Plus, she was devoted to making the gallery all that it could be. We were moving to a larger space in the mall, and she asked if she could come in extra early to prepare things for the move. That was very meaningful to me.

I have another business in St. Louis that was started by my father in 1960. It was a brick distributorship aimed at the architectural community for large commercial projects. I needed sales help there and Darlene was the perfect candidate, so I fired her from my gallery and hired her for Missouri Brick Company. She very quickly developed a strong following from the architectural community.

There are two very delightful anecdotes regarding Darlene.

We were driving in my car looking at a building to match the brick when Darlene asked about a large project that I was chasing for the brick selection. The project was the new St. Louis Cardinals

Stadium. I wanted to furnish it with every fiber of my being. Darlene asked me how many brick would be needed for the new stadium.

I responded, "You want a ballpark estimate?"

Ignoring that ultra-clever remark, she said, "Yes, how many brick will be needed?"

Once again, I asked, "You want a ballpark estimate?"

She said once again, "Yes, I do."

So I almost screamed, *"A ballpark estimate?"*

It finally dawned on her how clever a question that was. She made a gesture with her hand right over her head and said, "How could I have missed that?"

By the way, we received the order for the project and furnished 2.14 million brick for the construction of Busch Stadium III.

Another wonderful moment with Darlene is as follows. She was a great fan of my photography, and after viewing a couple of my latest images (Lew Portnoy taught me that if I called them images, I could charge more), she stated, "I don't understand why you aren't rich and famous. Your work is so great."

I said, "You know, Mozart died penniless!"

She said, "Yes, I know, but look how well he is doing now!"

GARFIELD, THE WONDER GOOSE

There was a wonderful restaurant in Clayton, Missouri, named the Leather Bottle, which had delightful lunch fare. It was an ideal place to take an architect to lunch, as they had a room that was filled with my hot-air balloon photos. I always felt somewhat special going there as they treated me very well. And no matter how crowded they were, they always seemed to find a table for me and my guests. The restaurant was owned by the Bland brothers, Kenny and Dick. They were both very bright, with Kenny being a world-class bridge player. The other brother, Dick, had a great sense of humor and loved pranks. One Christmas Eve, Dick and an architect friend of mine came to my house and brought me an unusual gift for Christmas.

I came home several hours later, and as I pulled in my driveway, my sons, Donny and Danny, came to greet me, saying, "Daddy, Daddy, you won't believe what we have."

Susan followed closely behind and said, "Don, we have a serious problem."

She led me to the basement door where down those steps to the basement was my workshop and my photographic darkroom. I walked into the workshop, and there tied to my radial arm saw was a large snow-white goose. I stepped into the workroom and skidded on my newly very slick floor. The goose relieved himself and started honking at me with an evil look in his eyes. This was Christmas

Eve, and they brought it to me for Christmas dinner. Susan had already named the damn thing "Garfield." How could we cook and eat something with a name? We had a walkway on the side of the garage that led to the back yard. There was a gate at the front, but no gate at the back, so I had to run to O. K. Hatchery to get some chicken wire to jerry-rig a goose pen. Just the thing I wanted to do on Christmas Eve. Big joke . . . thanks, guys.

Christmas came and went, and the goose became part of the family, apparently fairly comfortable in his runway on the side of our garage. Early one morning, a few days after Christmas, our phone rang, and it was our neighbor, Karen, who had a newborn, just a couple months old.

She said to me with total exasperation in her voice, breathing deeply between each word, and said, "Don, I haven't slept in days . . . the goose honks . . . the baby wakes and cries . . . the goose honks . . . the baby cries . . . the goose honks . . . you have got to do something."

I apologized and made another trip later that day to construct a goose pen in our backyard surrounding a fort that I built years earlier for the boys to play in. It was a fairly easy modification for this doggone goose. Garfield and I hated each other, and every time I came close, he would honk at me and I would honk back at him even louder.

We purchased an historic home that was built in 1850 in Old Kirkwood. One of my first tasks was back to O. K. Hatchery to purchase more chicken wire and supports for yet another goose pen. Each time I had to build another pen, I grew to despise that goose more and more. Susan, however, loved Garfield, and became known as the goose lady of our neighborhood. She cared for that goose daily, and the two of them, Susan and Garfield, became close friends. Garfield became our "guard goose." Anyone that came within fifty feet of our property was greeted with an eardrum-cracking *honk honk honk*. He probably scared off many bad guys, but probably many good guys as well. I always felt that when Ed McMahon came to our sidewalk to present me with my ten million dollars, he was driven away by the killer goose. I learned that snow geese live to around fifteen years or so, and midway of Garfield's sixteenth year, he sadly passed away. Susan asked me to take Garfield to Clark Animal Hospital to have his body cremated.

Ten days or so later, the phone rang, and it was Dr. Clark from his animal clinic telling me that Garfield was ready to be picked up. This opportunity only comes once in someone's life, so I placed my hand over the phone, called to Susan, and said, "Susan, your goose is cooked."

I thought that was much funnier than she did.

The Deutschland Experience

In 1982, I had an invitation to visit Gail Tile's manufacturing plant in Giessen, West Germany, and to attend the massive "Constructa Fair" in Hanover. I jumped at the opportunity for many reasons. The least of which was the fact that I had never been to Europe and a trip overseas was very enticing. I couldn't wait. Susan, who in her former life was a travel agent for a company in Denver specializing in European travel, mapped out a fabulous trip for me after my business part of the travel. She booked the nicest hotels for me in all of the key cities I would be visiting and said that I needed at least three weeks to see all the sights. My mom had always wanted to go to Europe, but my father had zero interest in leaving the United States. So I invited her to meet me in Nice and we would travel together. In principle, this was a terrific idea, but my mom snored with infinite decibels. So after one night of sleeping on the bathroom floor, two rooms were a necessity. The itinerary that Susan had mapped out for me was terrific. After the Germany meeting, Susan had arranged for a Eurail Pass, which was a first-class pass for all of the European railroads which was designed to encourage international travel. It had to be purchased in the USA. With Susan's travel arrangements, this was to be my trip of a lifetime. My stops included Heidelberg, Zurich in Switzerland, Milan in Italy, Nice in France (where I was meeting my mom at the airport), Venice, Florence, Geneva, Paris, and London before our flight back to St. Louis. More about this post-trip later.

Leaving Lambert Airport in St. Louis and waiting on the tarmac, there was a slight mist in the air, and the sky was very gray and gloomy at two o'clock in the afternoon. The flight was around eleven hours to Frankfurt, and thanks to my close friend, Dr. David Berland, as I was on the plane, I entered the time of the arrival city on my watch. Then, when that time dictated my normal sleep hour, I took a Halcion sleeping pill to force me to sleep on the destination city's time. It worked beautifully. I landed in Frankfurt well rested. Arnold Schneider (head of international business, who was fluent in five languages) met me at the airport, and we drove to Giessen. It was a short thirty-three-mile drive to the Steinsgarten Hotel where we met with the other invitees, Bud Morris from Portland, Oregon, Harry Atherton from Richmond, Virginia, Bob Klinges from Pittsburgh, Pennsylvania, and Arnold Mozes from Boston, Massachusetts (I think). Since we were all together, we went to the front desk and found a pile of room keys awaiting us. We all grabbed a key and squeezed into the teeny-tiny elevator to our respective rooms. I was very well rested (I thought) but fell asleep very quickly, only to be awakened by a phone call from my beautiful wife, Susan, who asked how the flight was and how rested I was. She then informed me that St. Louis had the largest snowfall in thirty years and was totally immobilized in twenty-two inches of snow. We spoke for a while, and then I went back to sleep. The next morning in the breakfast room, several of the Gail Tile travelers asked if my wife had gotten in touch with me last night. The hotel operator didn't know who grabbed which room key, so several rooms were contacted before Susan found me. They all remarked about the big snowfall and how nice my wife sounded. I then worried about that international phone call bill.

The Gail people treated us like royalty, and wined and dined us in the top restaurants in the area. One night we were hosted at a very old castle named Staufenberg's Castle in Durbach, Germany. We were ushered in and given the bill of fare on a parchment scroll. The meal was decided for us and it looked fabulous. The first course was garlic soup, which arrived at our table in a large bowl containing the blackest soup I had ever seen. It was incredibly delicious; however, with the principal ingredient being garlic, it was greatly odorific. For days, intense scrubbing in the shower failed to remove the pungent aroma emanating from our pores. Personal distancing ruled for several days thereafter.

Every night, we dined in a different first-class restaurant, mostly white tablecloth tables and served by tuxedoed waiters. The food was outstanding. Bill Klinges, who was of a fairly surly nature and had never been to Germany, kept saying that all he heard about German food was *sauerkraut*. How come he hadn't seen any sauerkraut? I felt this was a great insult to our German hosts who were treating us to absolutely delicious gourmet meals. I became aware that our Gail hosts considered "sauerkraut" a peasant food. It was some sort of an insult to the hosts who were treating us to very elegant Germanic cuisine.

We attended the Constructa Fair, which was an unforgettable experience with seven huge buildings devoted to construction materials. One building was entirely tile-related. The building trade fairs in the USA at that time were contained in one building, with small booths for vendors of various building materials to show their products. The U.S. shows generally were two to three days at most, which required exhibitors to display their wares in very quickly assembled displays that could be easily disassembled and packed away for the next trade show. Not so in Germany. The trade fairs last for two weeks or so, plus one entire week for preparation and construction, which allows for massive and very elaborate displays to be constructed. I was totally overwhelmed. Also, in the U.S. trade shows, that is exactly what occurs, a "show." There are lookers, but no business transacted. In the European shows, at least in Germany, business is actually transacted. Arnold Schneider said that as a rule, several million dollars of Gail Tile sales actually occurred during these shows. Quite different from our USA trade shows.

After our trade-show visit, we were then again returned to Giessen, where we were regaled with several wonderful dinners, but *no sauerkraut*! Bill Klinges continually complained. I considered it to be very rude to our hosts. Apparently, so did they.

On our last night in Giessen, we were taken to a very old, probably several hundred years old, heavily wooden paneled restaurant. We were seated at a long table, given menus, and placed our orders. Bill Klinges was seated at the head of one end of our table. All our food was delivered except for Bill Klinges's food. After several minutes, a very large silver platter with a large hog's head with wide open eyes resting on a large pile of *sauerkraut* was placed in front of Bill Klinges.

Arnold Schneider, our host for the trip, walked to the head of the table and at the top of his lungs shouted, "Here, Herr Klinges, is *your Goddamn sauerkraut!*"

SATURDAY MORNING
BREAKFAST

My friend, Lewis Portnoy, who was a great sports photographer and a longtime friend, was having breakfast every Saturday morning with a group of very successful photographers who worked for Anheuser-Busch, NBC Sports, Ralston Purina, PGA, Southwestern Bell, *Post-Dispatch*, and *Globe-Democrat* newspapers. I recently had success with my hot-air balloon graphics and was doing all of the photographs in the program for the Great Forest Park Balloon Race, so I had the credentials and was invited to join this elite group. That was in 1982, and believe it or not, that breakfast is still a Saturday morning event that had been going on for thirty-eight years. Members have come and gone, died, moved away, etc., but the event lives on.

Drew Karandjeff is one of the longer-tenured members and is a true perfectionist. Drew always has the best of whatever there is and will eagerly tell you why it is so perfect. He has several hotsy-totsy automobiles now, and in the past, had a Testarossa, an NSX, and several others of world-class quality. One morning, he told us that he had found the perfect detailer to work on cleaning his car and making it absolutely perfecto. All of us at breakfast were greatly impressed as usual. He informed us that this detailer was weeks behind, but he was fortunate to have found him as this detailer was the absolute best. As always, we saw it later after Drew's car of the moment was impeccably detailed, and indeed, Drew was right, the guy was very, very good.

I owned my first Lexus, which I referred to as being a childhood version, the Lexus ES, which stood for Economy Sedan. This car was a fabulous vehicle with a white exterior and beige leather interior. It was right at the top of vehicles that I had ever owned in my life. However, this was 1995, and my 1992 ES had 104,000 miles on it. It was time for a new one. There was no visible difference between the 1992 and the 1995, so I ordered the exact color combination as the 1992 since I loved it so. The new vehicle would be in in three to four weeks after I placed the order.

The next week at the Saturday morning breakfast, I informed the table, especially Drew, that I had found the absolute best detailer in the world and I made an appointment with him in about four weeks. Drew left early that morning, and I told everybody else that it was a prank and I had ordered a new car.

The dealer, Plaza Motors, informed me that my car had arrived and I could pick it up Friday evening, just in time for the Saturday morning breakfast. When I arrived, I ate breakfast and then announced to the table that my detailer had finished with my car and he did an incredible job. Drew couldn't wait to see it after breakfast. We all went to the parking lot to view my "detailed" car, and everyone just kept remarking how perfect a job it was. Drew kept looking at all sides, and even the tires had gloss on them.

I popped the trunk, and he said, "Wow, this guy is really great." I opened the driver's door and that brand-new car aroma hit us all in the face. He said, "Good grief, the carpet looks perfect and the leather seats have been totally refurbished. I can't believe how good this guy is."

Then, my friend, Lew Portnoy said, "Look, he even rolled back the odometer." It showed thirty-six miles on it. The jig was up, but what a *great* moment!

Susan thought for years that the only reason that I got exactly the same car was for that very moment when I *got* Drew.

She may have been right.

My Mother,
The Brilliant Lady

My mother was a very well-educated and very well-read lady. She loved crossword puzzles and had the remarkable ability to work the *New York Times* crossword puzzle in record time. She always used words in her everyday language that should have been left in books. I constantly had to ask her the meaning of a particular word that she was using for some everyday object. However, as an avid reader, she read *Valley of the Dolls* by Jacqueline Susan and said that it was the filthiest book she ever read.

She said, "There were so many dirty words in it. I didn't even know the meaning of most of them."

I said, "If you didn't know their meaning, how did you know they were dirty?"

She said, "Well, you could just tell."

My mom was indeed a brilliant lady who was always deep in thought. However, it was rarely about what she was doing at the time. If she were a professor, she could have been termed "absentminded." However, being just a schoolteacher, I would term her "scatterbrained."

We always had the latest newfangled items (my dad was a real sucker for those) and we were the first ones in the neighborhood to have that new thing called television. It was so exciting that our neighbors wanted to come over and see it. Word spread to people in the neighborhood that we had never met before, and soon our living room became an every-night venue for lots and lots of people, many of whom we had never met. My mom brought all the kitchen and dining room chairs for people to sit and watch our TV. After several weeks of this, one evening, my dad, on his way back to the TV room, had to step over a couple of people who were sitting on the floor and who we really didn't know at all.

My dad stood up and said, "Everybody, *out!*"

We also had, I think, one of the first dishwashers. At that time in the forties, there were no built-in dishwashers as far as I knew. Our dishwasher was a freestanding unit that was a round toploading white porcelain item on rollers that was hooked up to the kitchen-sink pipes by hoses. At some point, our dishwasher lost one of its castor rollers and was slightly tilted forward. On this particular evening, my brother, dad, and I were sitting at the kitchen table talking baseball (actually, they were talking and I was listening). Then, some time after dinner, my mom asked if we wanted some ice cream. Of course, we did. Mom had already placed the dinner dishes in the dishwasher, and it had just finished its cycle. The top of the washer was still very hot. Years ago, ice cream quarts came in "bricks," which were long rectangular boxes that you would open and slice the ice cream into squares for serving. My mom placed a serving platter on the slightly-askew dishwasher and started slicing the ice cream. My dad, after talking about one of Stan Musial's hits that day, looked over at the dishwasher and saw a slice of ice cream on the floor. He glanced up and saw another slice balancing on the edge of the platter. He saw it drop to the floor and land on top of the slice on the floor. He got our attention, and my brother and I looked up and saw another slice slowly, with the speed of a snail, make its way to the edge of the platter, teeter a moment, and then plop to the floor. We, my dad especially, always watched things develop with my mom without interrupting the occurrence, just to see how it would develop. My mom was happily slicing the brick when she glanced at the platter and saw just melted ice cream liquid. She looked down, saw the slices in a pile on the floor, and started laughing so hard that she had to excuse herself to change her dress.

Another time that my mother was deep in thought about something other than what she was doing at the time, was one day when my dad came home for lunch. My mom had cooked a couple of pork chops and placed one on a plate directly from the frying pan on the stove. She turned, and the pork chop slipped off the plate, skittered across the floor, and stopped just at the door to the basement. She then placed the plate on the table, not noticing that the pork chop was gone and with just a little grease remaining from the launched pork chop. She set it down in front my dad at the table and then turned back to the stove. My dad looked at the plate that had just a little grease and nothing else. Of course, he said nothing, wondering what would happen next. My mom turned and saw my dad's empty plate, thinking he was ready for another and not wondering how he ate the chop, bone and all. She picked up his plate, returned to the stove, and placed another pork chop on his plate. Now with the grease from two pork chops, the plate was even more slippery, and when she turned, the second pork chop slipped off the plate and slid within a couple of inches of the first one.

My dad said, "Aha, that's what happened."

My mom saw it and once again laughed so hard. It was time to change her dress again.

My Brother, Robert Marquess

Robert K. Marquess, whose middle initial stood for Kingsland, a forever kept name in our heritage, was called King by our family. My father's name was Robert Lee Marquess, so not to be confused with two Roberts in the family, my brother became King. (I learned much later in life that he hated that name and told everyone that his name was Bob.)

My brother was one of the smartest people I have ever known, but also the most frugal (cheapest) person I have ever met. He was also ten years older than me and considerably taller—he was almost 6 foot 5 inches. My brother's frugality caused him to never pay to park his car anywhere. He would prefer to find a spot on the street somewhere and walk the hundred or so blocks to whatever destination chosen. Needless to say, he would never valet his car because he would not consider giving the attendant a tip. As a matter of fact, I don't think he ever gave anyone a tip in his entire eighty-six years of life.

This may seem like a fabrication regarding my brother, but it is an absolute fact. He kept a book with him every day, recorded every penny spent during the day, and balanced before going to bed each night. He would purchase an occasional candy bar or jawbreaker for me, but never neglected to write it in his little book (jawbreaker, Don, 1 cent). I have very vivid memories of lying in bed as a three-to-four-year-old and hearing my father calling to my brother, "King, go to bed," with my brother responding, "I can't, I'm a nickel out."

My father would then say in louder more definite terms, "Go to bed, I'll give you the nickel."

My brother would respond, "I can't. If I'm a nickel out, I could be a dollar out."

My father would then say, "Go to bed . . . . *I will give you the nickel!*"

To further iterate my brother's frugality and brilliant reasoning abilities, I was probably three or four, with my brother being thirteen or fourteen, when we were all in the living room listening to the *Baby Snooks* radio show (Maybe not, but that was one of my favorites) when my mom and dad decided that chocolate malts would be a great thing for all of us to enjoy. My parents gave my brother the money and sent him to Ted Drewes Frozen Custard for four chocolate malts. My brother jumped on his bicycle and went to fetch. Sometime later, my brother came home to the backdoor in tears and said that something terrible had happened.

My mom and dad said, "What happened?"

My brother sobbingly said, "When I turned the corner on Mardel, Don's malt flew out of the basket and smashed into the gutter."

My mom said, "How did you know it was Don's chocolate malt? Did it have his name on it?"

My brother said, "No, it didn't, but you and Daddy paid for it. I went and got it . . . it just had to be Don's."

I remember that vividly. However, I didn't realize the humor in it until several years later. If I remember correctly, my mom got four glasses and made four malts from the three.

My brother became a prominent CPA in Shreveport, Louisiana, and married a lovely (and very understanding) lady named Millie. My brother still balanced his pocket money with daily expenditures before going to bed each night and convinced Millie to do so also. As Millie explained it to me, one night she was out about $15 or $16 and she couldn't remember what happened to it.

My brother said, "All right, now, think. You woke up this morning, and where did you go? Then what did you do?"

Millie started to think, then threw up her hands and said, "*I don't know, and I don't care. It is gone! I'm not doing this ever again!*"

Surprisingly, my brother accepted this, and the marriage did not end in divorce. (Lawyers cost money.)

When our parents died, my brother's part of the estate was our parents' home, with the contents to be split equally between us. Susan and I invited my brother and Millie to join us for dinner at our home.

When they arrived, my brother said to me, "I have great news for you. That colored spotlight thing that Mom and Dad had, I sold for forty dollars. Here is your twenty."

He gave me a bill and entered the kitchen to say hello to Susan. I looked at the bill and it was a ten, not a twenty.

I called to my brother and said, "You gave me a ten, not a twenty."

He said, "No, I gave you a twenty."

I repeated, "You only gave me a ten."

He reached in his pocket, pulled out his notebook, did some calculations, then opened his wallet, counted his bills, and said, "*You're right!*," and then gave me another ten. He was seventy-two at that time, still keeping his little notebook.

I have always equated intelligence with a sense of humor, and my brother, whose IQ was in the 150 territory, had a terrific sense of humor. He could tell a joke with the best of them and laugh uproariously when he heard a doozie. He was drafted into the army and truly thought that it was a colossal waste of time. He was a very strong patriot, believed strongly in our armed forces, and served his country in the 5th Army's Finance Corp. He just never thought of it as a lifetime commitment. He was selected for OCS (officer candidate school) but respectively declined. He told me that one of the only things he learned in the army was when the drill sergeant was explaining the functioning of the M1 rifle.

The sergeant said, "These two things happen simultaneously . . . one right after the other."

A fellow draftee and lifetime friend of my brother told me that the drill sergeant at Fort Riley, Kansas, got nose to nose with my brother and said, "Marquess, you are not a soldier now and you will never be one!"

My brother replied, "Thank you very much!"

WORLD-RECORD GAMBLING CONVERSATION

My son, Jeffrey K. Marquess, is an intelligent and well-educated individual with a degree in economics. However, he has a mental blockage when it comes to one certain thing—*gambling*!

We were in Florida on a business trip at the Peabody Hotel in Orlando when Jeffrey saw that the sport, JAI ALAI, was being played at a location not very far from our hotel. Jai alai is generally thought of as the fastest sport in the world, with the "pelota" (the ball) reaching speeds of 180 miles per hour. The ball is approximately three-fourth the size of a baseball and much harder. The center is made of hard Brazilian rubber and is handstitched very tightly with two layers of leather producing a ball so hard that after about twenty minutes or so of 180 mph pounding, it must be replaced by a new one. At any rate, the sole purpose of this sport is gambling, which made it very attractive to my son and, in all honestly, to me also.

Even in a sport totally unknown to either of us, Jeffrey instinctively knows who should win the game. He studies from the program, reads up on it, does his Jethro Clampett ciphering, and comes up with the best possible wager. Jeffrey always knows which player, horse, or dog should win. Sadly, that is not always who *does* win.

Without question, Jeffery is a most informed gambler. I, on the other hand, will pick a horse for its color or number, or the dog who appears to glance at me with a well-directed tail wag. I never intellectualize my wagers. Every so often my method works. I have a friend whose science at picking dog or horse possible winners is based solely on which animal relieves himself before the race. He feels that that makes the animal lighter and less stressful. Everyone has a system. Jeffrey's system is with pure intellectual logic as well as intense research. When his pick loses, evil lurks.

Our jai alai adventure went the wrong way for Jeffrey, and our (almost) never-ending discussion ensued.

I said, "Jeffrey, before you wager even a penny, you have to accept the possibility that there is a strong chance that you will not see that penny again. It is a fifty-fifty chance you are taking by risking that money."

"Dad, what do you mean fifty-fifty? What about the odds?"

"Jeffrey, either they keep that money or you get it back."

"Dad, have you ever had a class in statistics and probabilities? I have, and I think what you are saying defies the basic premise of probability."

"Jeff, *you* are denying the simple fact that you are risking the loss of whatever wager you make, and you have to accept that outcome before you place any bet on anything. You either get your wager back or they keep it."

"But Dad, there are the odds to consider. Don't you understand?"

"Jeffery, the odds are just the reward you receive for the likelihood of the occurrence. Think of it as a bonus you receive, but nevertheless, it is a fifty-fifty chance that you get your money back or they keep it."

"But Dad . . ., the odds are based on knowledge by the handicappers who make their living by studying past performances and wagering results in the past. Where do you come up with that stupid fifty-fifty statement? Do you think you know more than these great minds who make their living by creating the odds?"

I could see that this was a hopeless endeavor to get across my simple statement of you either get your money back or they keep it. It is a fifty-fifty chance. A bettor must accept the possibility of losing whatever he wagers. I felt maybe I could try another tack.

"Okay, Jeff, look at it this way, all bets are equal regardless of odds. And if an unlikely wager wins, think of the money you receive as a lagniappe that you receive for playing. The money you wager is the entertainment cost for the event. If you get it back, *hooray*. If you get it back with an award attached, a *greater hooray* is realized. Either way, it is a fifty-fifty chance of receiving your money back or they keep it."

"But Dad . . . smart bets usually win."

"Jeff, that is not the point at all. My point is that before you risk your money, you must accept the possibility of the loss. If you can't afford the risk, don't play. It *is* a fifty-fifty proposition."

At this point of our discussion, we had reached our hotel room, and I was ready for sleep time.

I turned off the lights and rolled over on my king-sized bed.

The lights came back on, and Jeffrey said, "But Dad, think about this . . . ."

I said, "Jeff, you think about this . . . I no longer care. Goodnight!"

"But Dad . . . ."

I replied, "Zzzzzzzzzzzzzzz."

Bill Haslett and
The Las Vegas Caper

Most people are concerned with quality to a certain degree, but there are some people who are obsessed with quality to the utmost degree. My friend, Bill Haslett, is over the top in quality obsession. He cared greatly about the material used in shirts, jackets, and shoes, and in cars, it had to be a Lexus. Bill demanded perfection in most everything.

In 1990, there was a CTDA (Ceramic Tile Distributors of America) convention in Anaheim, California, that we both would be attending. Bill's office was in New Jersey, and mine was in St. Louis. With both of us loving Las Vegas and with the lure of the blackjack tables, we decided that it would be a great stop for a couple of days on our way to Anaheim. We had decided to meet in front of the white tiger's area at the Mirage Hotel shortly after our arrivals. Bill was staying at the Tropicana, while I had a luxurious (standard) room at the Mirage. Bill, the perfectionist, met me at exactly 2 p.m. as scheduled. After the usual greetings of how our individual flights were and our room accommodations, Bill showed me his new business card that was specially designed for him by a highly respected firm in Atlanta. He pointed the special font that was used as well as the perfect deep red shade of burgundy on the ecru-colored card stock. He kept flipping the corner of the card, remarking about the thickness of the stock. We then walked through the casino seeking a blackjack table with the best-looking female dealer. We found a hot one at fifteen-dollars-minimum table and sat down to play. At that moment, the dealer was so great-looking that I don't think it mattered at the time to either of us whether we won or lost. Bill took out his card again and passed it over to me again to look at it again and asked me to comment on the quality of the card stock, font, selection, and color of the printing. He asked the dealer what she thought, then he asked me to pass it to the player next to me for his comment. Bill was over the top regarding his new card. At dinner that evening, he passed the card to me once again for inspection. He also asked our waitress what she thought about the card. No question, it was the "card of the century," but I had way too much of that business card and I didn't want to hear about it anymore.

We played blackjack most of the next day and did not adversely affect the coffers of the Mirage. I checked out of my room while Bill and I hailed a cab and headed to Hertz to pick up the car I preordered. The temperature in Las Vegas was a toasty 112 degrees. People say you don't feel it as much because of the low humidity. Not so. It was scorching. As planned, we were to pick up the car, then go to the Tropicana, check Bill out of his room, then make the drive to Anaheim.

Everything was going to plan . . . until the counter person at Hertz said, "Sorry, Mr. Marquess, we don't have the car you reserved".

I said, "What? You can't be serious. I ordered and paid by credit card for a Cadillac."

I guess I shouldn't have made such a big deal about it, but a really nice car for the drive to Anaheim was a necessity. The clerk was being very nice, but I was being a real jerk. After a very heated and immature attitude on my part, I told him just where he could put the substitute car and stormed out of the office . . . directly into the stifling heat . . . and no cab to be seen anywhere. It was hotter than hell, and we had no way of getting anywhere.

Bill said, "Well, you showed them, didn't you?"

In 1990, the Hertz Car Rental was pretty far off the strip with no possibility of catching a cab. Considerably away, we saw an Alamo

Car Rental across the road and past the bridge underpass, and we lugged (never before was the word luggage more appropriate) my suitcase, camera bag, and gear to the Alamo office. The temperature at this time was, I'm certain, around 180 degrees. The Alamo office was a stroke of luck in that they had a fairly new Lincoln that they wanted to go back to their Anaheim office. What an absolute stroke of luck! It was actually less costly than that stinking Cadillac at Hertz.

We then drove to the Tropicana to check Bill out of his room, I gave the valet $5 just to hold the car until we got back downstairs. In Bill's room, I saw his box of those world-class business cards. I picked up the box and concealed it in my hand behind a small airline carry-on bag of Bill's, and we went downstairs to get the car and start the drive to Anaheim. I secretly hid his business cards behind the passenger seat and said nothing to Bill. We started our four-hour drive to the CTDA convention in Anaheim. Bill and I were very good friends and enjoyed the ride.

The Alamo Anaheim office was closing at 6 p.m., and we arrived in plenty of time at 5:30 p.m. or so. The young lady at the counter was very nice and friendly and asked if the car was full of gas. I said no, it wasn't. Then she said that they would charge $4.25 per gallon, and it would be best if we would drive a couple of miles up the road to fill up. She said that she had a barbecue to go to and would have to leave, but when we come back to leave the car at the gate, drop the key, and contract through the slot in the door, and she would call a cab for us to be waiting when we returned. How great was that! She was not only good-looking but greatly efficient and accommodating. We filled the tank and returned to the rental office, and there waiting for us was the promised cab. We loaded the luggage in the cab, but I totally forgot all about Bill's cards and told him what I had done. He was ashen. I promised to call them in the morning and pay for a courier to deliver the cards to our hotel. He felt better about it after I told him that I would fix the prank, and I think he actually thought it was funny.

Waiting for them to open the next morning, my wife, Susan, called me and said that Alamo called and wanted to know my hotel and room number in Anaheim. She gave it and said that I should expect a call.

The call came! Alamo wanted to know why I didn't leave the car at the gate under the canopy. I said I did leave the car and all of the paperwork along with the key that was dropped through the slot in the door per instructions. They thought I still had the car. I gave them Bill Haslett's room number to call for verification. Ten minutes later, I received a call from their home office wanting to hear my story again. A few minutes after that, I received another call from their insurance specialist asking for details. The car was *stolen!* And I was the primary suspect.

Bill called after realizing that if the car was stolen, so were his business cards. Whether I would be doing time for car theft didn't matter. His cards were all that mattered.

This story does have a happy ending, at least for me. The car apparently was stolen, but since I left the key in the envelope with the paperwork, I was no longer a suspect. Bill contacted his wife in New Jersey, and she FedExed the other box of his cards, which he received the next morning. Fortunately, Bill and I remained friends.

LINDA ZORSCH

Susan and I were living in what we considered a luxury apartment in General Grant Colonial Village in suburban St. Louis. It contained two bedrooms and a very large recreation room on the lower level. We felt we had hit the big time. Pat and Linda Zorsch, our new upstairs neighbors, had just moved in and seemed to want to make friends with us. Pat Zorsch, the husband, was a tall (six feet) slender CPA who was a friendly sort and he wanted to socialize with us. His wife, Linda, was a moderately attractive brunette who was a stay-at-home wife. Linda was of normal build, probably around five feet five inches and mostly slender with one major exception—she had the largest breasts that neither Susan nor I had ever seen before. We knew that her chest had to have set some sort of breastal record. When you stood face to face with Linda, you had to give an extra couple of feet or so distance so as not to brush up against those two whoppers.

Susan and I had several close friends that would come over with regularity for dinner and charades, clue, Monopoly, or some other enjoyable game. At some point in the evening, the subject of our upstairs neighbors would come up. Both of our guests (the guys especially) would find it an intriguing bit of information regarding Linda's breasts, and not completely believing our descriptions, would ask to meet her and her accountant husband. I would call upstairs and invite them down to meet our friends. They would arrive, and we would all make small talk for a while. Then I would go to the kitchen to freshen drinks or get chips or something, and one of our friends would get up to assist.

As soon as we rounded the kitchen wall, a very animated, yet totally silent reaction as our guest mouthed, "My God, I can't believe it."

Exaggerated hand gestures extended as far as the arms can reach were given as the reaction to the enormity of Linda's chest. Husband Pat, the stereotypical CPA, was either unaware of our attitude or way too nerdish to think much about it. He assumed that we invited them as friends. I guess that sounds very cruel and heartless, but her breasts overshadowed all other considerations. Pat and Linda may have been an interesting couple, but thoughts beyond her breasts were nonexistent.

Like many apartment buildings, the tenants' mailboxes were clustered on the first-floor hallway close to the entrance to the building. One Saturday, Pat Zorsch and I were retrieving our mail at the same time and started a casual conversation regarding our summer plans. I told Pat that we were planning a trip to New England (Susan's birth area) and the usual day trips to interesting local attractions (Cardinals baseball mostly).

He started his litany of summer plans: "I'm going to summer camp in July, going to a CPA seminar in early August, then Linda is having her operation, then . . . . "

I interrupted him in midsentence, "Linda is having an operation? For what?"

He, with a very serious look, said to me, "You may have noticed that Linda has very large breasts . . . " (I was trying very hard to keep a straight face, although his "you may have noticed" statement was causing internal hemorrhaging of my explosive laughter.) Then he continued, " . . . and she is having terrible backaches (I guess!) due to the size of them, and it is causing her to bend over from the weight of carrying them. So she is having 74 percent removed from her right breast and 60 percent from her left one."

Again, trying with great difficulty to be serious and quieting my giggle urge, I said, "What are they doing with the overage?," thinking that would cause a smile on his face or maybe even a chuckle.

He just looked at me for a moment and, in typical nerdlike fashion, said, "I don't know, I never asked. I assume they are just throwing it away."

That did it for me. I was about to explode. I turned to my apartment door, and as I was going in, I said, "Keep me abreast."

I told Susan as soon as I got in, and we both tried very hard to keep our laughter as quiet as possible. The ceiling was thin, and we didn't want them to hear us.

Boarding House Audi

Susan, the gorgeous lady I was married to for forty-two years and who greatly resembled Joan Collins, was a great admirer of fine automobiles, especially the high-performance fast ones. She drove a Jeep Station Wagon but longed for a "real performance automobile," and she especially loved Audi's. We lived close to an Audi dealer in Kirkwood, so I went and checked out the available cars in stock. I can't remember the exact model I found, but there was a really nice one that was a deep green, maybe olive green, that had a powerful engine, leather upholstery, and a great sound system, all wrapped up in a "real performance machine." I loved Susan beyond sensibility, so I bought that car (much more than I could afford) for my beautiful Susan. She was ecstatic. We took delivery of the car Friday afternoon, and she drove it all around the neighborhood. I seem to remember hearing her singing some sort of *vroom-vroom* song from blocks away. She was totally enraptured. That evening, we had made reservations at a very popular restaurant called the Jefferson Avenue Boarding House, and our best friends, Pat and Barry Oxenhandler, were meeting us at our house and we were taking them in the "driving machine" to dinner with us. I need to tell you that Susan, my beautiful Susan who loved high-performance cars, never had and never would drive on any highway anywhere, anytime. She felt (probably rightfully so) that her depth perception would be a danger to herself and anyone else on the highway. However, that didn't prevent her from instructing me how to drive on any highway or any thoroughfare for that matter. The Jefferson Avenue Boarding House required about ten miles of highway driving, so I was our pilot.

We arrived at the restaurant and pulled up to the front door, and the valet came to park our car.

I gave him the keys and said, "Drive carefully . . . this is a performance car. Be very careful and very respectful."

Susan echoed my instructions. We went in and ordered our gourmet meals. I excused myself after ordering, purportedly to hit the bathroom and seek the manager. The manager, who was also the owner, had, in addition to magnificent cuisine, a rather delightful sense of humor.

I met with him out of sight of our table and said to him, "As we are finishing our desserts, I will ask the waiter to have the valet bring the car to the front door for us. He should look a little puzzled and go to find you. You will come to our table and say, 'Sir, I am very sorry, we don't have valet parking.'"

He thought that was a delightful prank for my wife's new Audi, so the plan was put in place. I went back to the table just before the appetizers arrived and then enjoyed our delicious meal. Susan had lamb cooked in some sort of mint sauce, and I will never forget the fabulous calf's liver "something or other" that I had. It was spectacular. We ordered desserts, and per plot, I requested the waiter to inform the valet to fetch our car. He looked puzzled (as planned) and went away.

Then the owner came up as planned, wearing a very sad puzzled look and said, "Sir, I'm very sorry, we don't have valet parking."

Susan's face went through many expressions. First surprise, then confusion, then anger, then absolute rage, saying, "My God . . . we just gave my new car away to some thief!"

The owner knuckled under immediately, pointed at me, and said, "He made me say that . . . we do have valet parking, and your car is waiting at the front door!"

It is difficult to describe laughing rage, but Susan had it. She was so relieved knowing that it was my harmless prank and she really still had her "driving machine." The ride home at first was kind of quiet.

Then she said, "Just you wait, Henry Higgins, just you wait." Then she smiled and said that she knew why she loved me. (That fact had always puzzled me.)

The Killer Stalactite

The time on the "killer clock" with its sound-deafening *tick tock* showed 10:30 p.m. when a knock on our dorm-room door banged loud enough to almost out-volume the clock. So I opened the door to find Ed Warnol, our down-the-hall neighbor, announcing that a trip to the Minute Inn for Matty's incredible chili was happening and did we want to ride along. Matty's chili was legendary, and any evening would be gleefully interrupted with a trip for her gourmet (?) red bean spicy beef chili containing garlic, red and yellow peppers, along with a semilethal dose of cayenne pepper. Once tried, never refused. So Ed Warnol, my roommate Roger, and me along with Tom Brooks from down the hall all got into Ed's car and headed toward the Minute Inn. This was late November, the day after a significant snowfall occurred, but the sky was crystal clear and appeared to have about eight billion or so brightly twinkling starts. The temperature was somewhat south of freezing, but Ed's car was nice and toasty. The sun during the day had caused the melting of the snow and created giant icicles hanging on the eaves of the houses, and most of them were quite impressive.

Matty's chili was indeed a bowl of wonder, and we all had at least two bowls. Then as we headed back to Hyde House Hall F, we passed by the most incredible icicle we had ever seen. It was hanging on the side of a garage with a top measurement approaching three feet. That sucker was over six feet from top to bottom and probably weighed sixty pounds or so. Ed Warnol's roommate was sort of a creepy individual who never said much and had a turtlelike appearance as he walked with his head tucked very closely to his shoulders. He wore thin-rimmed glasses halfway down his nose with his beady dark eyes peeking over the top of the glasses. His pastime was cave exploring. He was a *spelunker.* His name was Ed Bardett and he was very unsociable and appeared to have very little personality, if any at all. His favorite record was an album titled *The Sounds of Sebring,* which had nothing but the sounds of engines as they rounded the track. No Elvis, Johnny Cash, or Julie London. Being a spelunker, there was no doubt that this mammoth icicle was a stalactite that needed to be Ed's gift.

The four of us stopped the car, got out, and tried our best to remove the icicle from the roof's edge. That chunk of ice must have weighed fifty-plus pounds and was taken down with great care. The icicle was so big that it wouldn't fit in the car, so I in the front and Roger in the back seat carefully held the prize outside the car, as Ed Warnol drove very carefully back to our dorm. We parked the car and with great care carried the icicle up the stairs to our second-floor hallway. Ed Warnol and I carried the stalactite down the hall to Ed's room. Ed opened the door, and his roommate was sound asleep in his bed. Roger came in and gently folded back the bed cover of Ed's bed. Ed Warnol and I very carefully set the icicle next to the sleeping Ed. We tiptoed out of the room, closed the door quietly, and waited for the scream. As discretely as possible, we knocked on most of the doors and told our dorm mates of our caper. Ten or so of the guys came out, and we all huddled around the door waiting to hear the spelunker screaming as he discovered his gift. We waited in gleeful anticipation. Nothing at first . . . then nothing at second. We kept waiting, nothing. Slowly, one by one, our dorm mates returned to their rooms giving up. Roger, Tom, Ed, and I would not give up. We still waited. After almost an hour, Roger and I gave up and went back to our room. Ed said goodnight and told us that we would probably hear the wild scream that would wake us up sometime in the middle of the night. Still *nothing*!

Probably the greatest prank of the year fell flat. Very disappointing! The dorm had a gang shower and bathroom at the end of the hallway, and there in the shower the next morning was Ed Bardett soaping himself up as if nothing happened.

Egad. One of the dorm mates said to Ed, "How did you sleep last night, Ed?"

Ed replied, "Someone put a big chunk of ice in my bed last night. I woke up around three and put it in the shower."

Over the corner of the shower was the melting three-foot hunk of ice. There was no further emotion from the spelunker. *Bummer!*

So sad, so very, very sad.

Breeders' Cup Gambit

My son, Jeffrey, loved horse racing and the thrill of the wager. The simulcast of the 1985 Breeders' Cup was at Fairmount Park, which was just across the Mississippi from St. Louis, so we planned to attend. We made a reservation at the Black Stallion room, which had a very nice buffet and monitors galore. The one-mile race (I think there were seven or eight races in total) had a great-looking gray horse named Cozzene. It fit right in with my highly scientific method of horse selection for any race. Bet the gray horse! I guess the real reason is that as you look at all of the horses rounding the track, it is very easy to spot the gray horse and to see his position in the group. At racetracks, the betting windows have very creative in ways you can wager. There are flat bets where you can pick a horse to finish first, second, or third. Then there's an option called the exacta, where you pick the horses that finish first and second. Then there's the most difficult wager of all, where you pick the three horses that finish first, second, and third. The racetracks have devised many different ways that the bettor can structure his wager, many of which confuse me. However, one way I do understand is "boxing horses." It is possible in a trifecta race to "box" three horses for six dollars, which will result in half of the payout of the winning amount. This figure is generally a very big payout for the winning tickets due to the difficulty of picking three horses that finish first, second, and third. The higher the odds on the individual horses, the bigger the reward. There is another method of betting the trifecta and that is to "box" four horses, and three of those four horses must finish 1st (win), 2nd (place), and 3rd (show); however, this wager costs $24. I wagered the $24 and picked and boxed four horses.

The race was off, and the easily seen gray horse, Cozzene was easy to spot on the monitor. It looked like my individual bet ($20) on him was going to win. A couple of the other horses of my four chosen looked like they were strong possibilities to finish in the top three. The race ended with the gray Cozzene winning, and one of the other horses I picked finished second. Sadly, the horse I selected to finish third finished fourth. There goes my $24 on that bet. *But wait*, there's more. An inquiry sign was flashing on the tote board involving the third and fourth finishers. It seemed like an eternity, but they eventually disqualified the third (show) horse and bumped up my horse for my winning trifecta. The payout for the trifecta showed $867.950. I thought that is terrific, I get $433.475 . . . wait a minute, that is three digits after the decimal point; there should be only two. The payout was actually $8,679.85. I was getting half. Incredible! I was paid in cash for $4,339.75. What a win! There were still two or three races to go.

The next race was fast approaching, and Jeffrey and I were in the line leading up to the betting window when Jeffrey said to me, "Who are you betting in the next race, Dad?"

I responded, "I like the name Pebbles, I am betting her."

Jeffrey said, "How much are you betting on her, Dad?" I told him $20. Then Jeffrey says in a very loud voice, *"With all that money in your pocket!* You are only betting $20?"

I could hear all of the eyeballs in the room snapping in my direction. At the time, I felt that everyone at Fairmount Park had a prison record and carried a knife. My life was probably over. I could have strangled Jeffrey. Anyway, Pebbles won, and I added another $400 to my winnings. I was heavily loaded with close to $5,000, and this was Saturday and the banks were closed. No ATMs. We had a dinner date that night with friends, and I was afraid to leave the money at home knowing that the house could burn down and my money would go up in flames, so I just kept it in my pocket for the evening. I truly had the feeling that everyone we saw in Union Station (it was very crowded) while we were walking to Dierdorf and Hart's restaurant could tell by looking at me that I had $5,000 in my pocket and they were plotting to take it from me. I charged our portion on my credit card because I didn't want to reveal the wad I was carrying.

I was first in line at the drive-up window at Bank of America Monday morning.

Susan, Donny, Danny, and I had a wonderful week at the Polynesian Hotel in Disney World with the special meal and hotel program that cost $2,800, which we paid in cash thanks to Cozzene and his fellow racers. The balance of my $5,000 win is still drawing interest.

My Grandfather - The Indestructible

My maternal grandfather, Albert F. Froussard, was born in 1883 and died in 1984 at the age of 101. He was an inventor and received his fifteenth patent when he was eighty years old. He was a charter member of the Power Engineers' Association in St. Louis and sat on the review board for future applicants. When I was eight years old or so, my granddaddy was explaining some mechanical thing that he was working on and he was very impressed that I understood. I truly don't remember what it was or if I really understood what he was explaining, but from that moment on, he felt that I was the only one of his descendants that had any sense at all. My grandfather started his machine company named Multiple Boring Machine Company in 1917, and during the Second World War, he had sixty-five machinists working for him. My father, my mother (his daughter), my brother, and I all worked for my grandfather at one time or another. I was in charge of assembling the pages and binding them for his catalogues. I also was in charge of addressing and mailing his yearly calendars. I felt very privileged and important to have such a responsible position when I was ten years old or so during my summer vacations from school. I got paid also! Whenever the minimum wage requirement raised, I got a raise, always bringing my hourly wage up to the minimum. My granddad, in addition to being a brilliant inventor of machinery, was also very frugal. He always paid me the minimum wage. The catchphrase for my grandfather was, "He had all of his assets tied up in cash!"

Many people would come into Multiple Boring to see Albert F. Froussard, but the only way to meet with him was for the guest to go anywhere in his sixty-thousand-square-foot building, three-sectioned shop, stand there and wait, and in ten minutes or so my grandfather would pass by. He was always a hands-on boss who continuously checked on the jobs in process.

There is a story about him seeing one of his machinists in the shop and saying to him, "What are you doing?"

The man replied, "I'm helping Shaefer."

My grandfather approached Shaefer and said to him, "What are you doing?"

Shaefer replied, "I'm not doing anything."

My grandfather then fired "Shaefer's helper" saying, "Schaefer can do nothing without your help!"

Several visits with the machinists' union representative occurred shortly thereafter.

One of A. F. Froussard's many patented inventions was a portable boring bar that was used to remove the calcium deposits and suck them out of boilers on large ships. My grandfather would rent out these bars and a machinist to do the work while the ship was at sea. Prior to his invention, the ships would have to be in dry dock and immobilized for several weeks. His invention enabled the ships to keep sailing while the boiler was maintained.

My grandad rarely paid attention to allocation requirements during the Second World War. He somehow or another got just what he needed to complete whatever piece of machinery was necessary for his participation in the war effort. However, there were certain restrictions on many items that my grandfather just ignored. One day, a government man came to the shop with a letter stating that my grandfather had violated many of the material restrictions. My father at the time was my grandfather's accountant and was in the office working on the books. However, he had developed some allergic rash and had several facial splotches.

My grandfather yelled at the government inspector and said, "Look what you have done to my son-in-law, you have given him hives!"

He then picked up the inspector by the scruff of the neck and threw him physically out of the building and onto the sidewalk. My dad was certain that that was going to be the end of my grandfather's business. Two weeks later, a letter arrived that was very nicely written and appreciative for Albert F. Froussard's efforts during the war, however, with the cautionary request to pay more attention to allocation restrictions. That was all. Whew!

My grandfather's machinery company was highly respected in the industry and had the reputation of being a precision shop. My grandad was in his mid-eighties when a large bell-shaped iron casting was tooled and ready to be shipped to the customer. The truck was next to the machine that had finished the product. As always, my grandfather had his trusty micrometer with him and measured it only to discover that it was one thousandth of an inch off. He would never permit anything to leave from his shop that was not up to his standards. He told the machinist to rework it to make it perfect. The bell had been prepared and ready to ship, but it was disconnected from the machine. The machinist, who had been with my grandfather for over thirty years, got very nervous about his error and restarted the machine without refastening the item and making it secure. The bell-shaped object slid off the machine and crushed my grandfather against the truck, doing serious damage to the truck as well as breaking many ribs and causing severe internal bleeding for my grandfather. He was rushed to the hospital, and when the family heard about it, we had all assumed that tragic accident would take his life. I was elected to spend the night with my grandmother at her home to be with her and comfort her through this tragedy. My grandad was in a coma for five days, and we all thought his life was over. The family members all took turns staying in his hospital room hoping he would recover. I was in the room when he awoke from the coma. His eyes fluttered a little, and he saw me in the room.

He said, "Don, it is a damn good thing that happened to me because it would have killed anyone else!"

He probably was right. He lived for 101 years.

Beautiful Virginia Beach

I was thirteen years old in 1954, and my dad had a very luxurious 1949 Lincoln Cosmopolitan just itching for a highway driving vacation. This car was referred to by my friends as "a boat." That Lincoln was almost eighteen-and-a-half-feet long and had a very luxurious and very comfortable interior. Just great for sleeping in the back seat (at thirteen, I couldn't think of other backseat activities). My dad and mom loved driving vacations. My dad had a recommendation from a friend that Virginia Beach was beautiful, and his friend even suggested a great hotel named Ocean Terrace that was right on the beach. I had never been to the ocean and was eagerly stoked for the adventure. The trip took us through the Blue Ridge Mountains of Virginia (that really had a "blue ridge" of fog on the top), and my dad couldn't stop talking about the great power of that Lincoln and kept saying how it "just walked" up those mountain roads. I felt that we were truly special in that fancy-smanchy automobile.

We arrived at the Ocean Terrace Hotel, went to our "luxurious" room, jumped into our swimming suits, and headed for the beach, which was just a few steps from our hotel. The beach was crowded on this very sultry July afternoon, and the ocean was just flat incredible for me to see. We found an open spot on the beach, laid out our towels, and headed for the surf. I have a very clear and embarrassing memory of my mom in her two-piece (just purchased for our trip) swimsuit that had a bright orange top. My mom was the first one in the ocean, and a giant wave hit her, knocked that orange top down, and revealed her naked breasts. Egad! She was greatly surprised and replaced it quickly. My dad didn't even see it.

I went into the ocean for the first time in my life and soon realized that swimming was a hopeless task until you went past the breaking waves. I was not a great swimmer, but an accomplished one, and managed to get past those breaking waves and take my first swim in the Atlantic Ocean. It was a totally different sensation than swimming in the close chlorinated swimming pool where my dad took me on many weekends, but I was loving the adventure. There were no sightings of sharks or stingrays, but I knew they were lurking for an attack. After an exciting fifteen minutes or so, I attempted to swim back to the beach, but a big wave caught me and just propelled me back to the sand. I felt that I had safely avoided those ocean predators that were planning on me for lunch.

I found our spot on the beach were my mom and dad were waiting and reclining on the towels. The sky was greatly overcast and the sun never made an appearance. What beautiful white skies of Virginia Beach! We got comfortable on our towels and coated ourselves with Coppertone oil. I will always remember that photo on the bottle of that partially covered little buttock showing that little child's tan line. We had been clouding ourselves on the beach for an hour or so when a lifeguard came up and said that we were out on the beach too long and we could get sunburned. How could that be possible with zero sun? I thought at the time the lifeguard was trying to sell us an umbrella or some sort of sun protection.

My dad saw the same ruse and said, "We are just fine, we have suntan lotion," and sent the lifeguard back to his canopied beach chair. Later, I realized that the suntan oil was just like basting the Thanksgiving turkey in the oven.

After four hours or so on the overcast sunless beach, while still in our swimsuits (Mom actually was all in hers), we went to a drugstore across the street from our hotel to get some treats and postcards to send to the landlubbers back home. I saw my mom looking at a postcard spinning rack. I looked away for a moment, turned back, and my mom was not there. I saw a clerk rushing over to pick up a lady on the floor and it was my Mom! She passed out in the middle of the store. My dad and I rushed over as the clerk was helping my mom to her feet. She said she was okay and had just gotten very dizzy and must have passed out.

We helped her back to the room, and she kept saying, "I'm okay, I just got dizzy."

We got in the room and helped my mom onto the bed.

Then my dad said, "I feel very strange," and then he passed out.

He laid on the floor for what seemed like an eternity to me and then got up on his bed. My mom said that she was feeling better and was very hungry that she would love a tuna salad sandwich. She had seen a deli a block or so from our hotel. She gave me some money and sent me on my way to get several of them. I felt very energized, and at thirteen, I felt I could save my parents and fetch those chilled tuna salad sandwiches. I was also thinking way back in the recesses of my mind what happens if they don't fully recover. I exited the back of the hotel, ran across the lawn, hurtled a hedge . . . and passed out. I laid there for a while and then made it to the deli to get the sandwiches. I brought them up to the room and knocked on the door, and a man I had never seen before answered the door. He was a doctor. My dad had called the hotel desk, and they sent a doctor to the room. My parents had sunstrokes. The lobster red of their skin sent me to the bathroom mirror to look at my face, and yep, I looked the same. We all had sunstrokes, and what the doctor called "sun poisoning." An afternoon on the beach ruined our trip to beautiful Virginia Beach.

After eight days of recovery in our room, we packed our luggage, had the bellman take it to our car, and tried to get in the car with our blazing red bodies. We, during our week of rest and drinking gallons of fluids, went through countless jars of Noxzema cream. We learned that Noxzema relieved the pain for about three minutes, then it caked and veined, and had to be reapplied, but it was the only thing that helped even a little bit. We could not put our clothes on and remained in our swimsuits for the trip home. The tendons in our legs stiffened and tightened up, so we could barely walk. We looked like crippled homeless lobsters going into a restaurant. I always lagged behind. My parents explained to the diners that we weren't crippled, we were just sunburned.

My skin peeled about three layers, and I developed three fluid-filled blisters on my upper right thigh. For anyone who cares to look, I still have three scars from those blisters, and my legs became badly infected.

My father's remark telling the lifeguard that we would be okay because "we have suntan lotion" still rings in my ears!

PROM NIGHT, 1958

At Bishop DuBourg High School in 1958, prom night was a *big deal*, as I guess it was in every school in the country at that time. It certainly was a big deal in 1958. I loved my high school years and was madly in love (I guess back then it was more "in lust" than "in love") with a super intelligent girl named Joan Eichenseer (pronounced "I can see her," just imagine all of the high school comments regarding that name). We had been together (going steady) for two years, and this was the big deal, *the senior prom*! Our group of friends, I guess, were considered nerds because none of us drank alcohol, did drugs, or anything really wrong except we were all very strong on romantic intimacies. We always had to park the car in very remote places at night after dinner and a movie. Everyone in our group was constantly an honor roll participant; however, my Joan blew all the rest of us away. She never shied to the "B" roll, always "A."

As a further description of our social group, one night I had my daddy's beautiful, but garish, orange and white Ford Victoria, with Joan and I in the front and two other couples squeezed in the back seat. We had gone to a movie at the Fox and afterwards took the long way home through Forest Park, where there was a very secluded road behind the St. Louis Art Museum. I made a joke that the car was running strangely and said that I needed to stop. It was a very private and empty road.

I said, "Gee, what should we do now?," knowing full well that loving and kissing was on all of our minds.

121

Larry's date, Margie, then said, "I know. Let's say a rosary."

That was the worst mood breaker I could ever remember. The car seemed to have no mechanical problems after that remark, so we headed home.

This prom night was anticipated to be truly memorable since it was our graduation year, and it meant that after we all went off to college, an era was ending. Larry Giesing took his Beverly Shea, Jim Sullivan (1957 graduate) and Dolores Meyer, Jim Coombs and Margie Brandhorst, along with Joan and me. This was a big, big night. Just as a little insight to our group, for Christmas that school year, I gave Joan a cashmere sweater, Larry gave Beverly a bracelet, Rich gave Margie a necklace, and Jim gave Dolores . . . a subscription to *Reader's Digest*. Dolores was totally embarrassed to tell everyone what gift she received. Jim Sullivan, always the practical individual, defended his gifting by saying that every month she would be reminded of how much he loved her. That was Jim, ever so sensible. So, anyway, this night was the night of nights for us. Jim made reservations for the eight of us at a moderately expensive restaurant named Steiney's Inn situated on the banks of the Meramec River. He secured a table in a private room overlooking the "scenic" (?) Meramec River. It really made no sense because at midnight after the prom, it would be very dark and no "scenic" was to be seen.

We all arrived in two cars just after 11:30 p.m., and our white tablecloth table was ready for us. All of the guys were in rented tuxedos and the girls were beautifully adorned in their special prom dresses. As I recall, Joan's was a light lime green kind of taffeta thing that had the beautiful orchid corsage (set me back eight bucks). I don't recall the others except the beautiful white formal dress that Dolores was wearing. It was made of some sort of white satin along with white fluffy cheesecloth material. Her dress won the prize of the evening. She was wearing a very tasteful wrist corsage (I had never seen one of those before), and with her high heels, she was close to five feet eleven. Her long brunette hair made her a striking young lady for certain.

We all placed our orders, which were all steaks, as Steiney's was well known for steaks. This dinner was definitely setting me back, close to twenty-five bucks, but what the hell, it was prom night. The tuxedoed waiter delivered our steaks, and an incredible culinary experience was about to occur. The steaks looked fantastic. Dolores ordered a filet mignon (the most costly on the menu). She took her knife out to cut it, but it caught the steak, and it slid it off the plate, on to her dress, and down to the floor. Jim didn't see it happen. He just looked at Dolores's plate and saw just a trace of grease but no steak!

He said to Dolores, "Where is your steak?"

Dolores, now completely mortified, said, "Jim, don't worry about it."

He said, "What do you mean don't worry about it? That steak cost $11.50. What happened to the steak?"

"Jim, just forget it."

"I won't forget it. What happened?"

"It slipped off my plate and fell to the floor."

Jim screamed, "What? It fell to the floor? . . . Are you serious?"

He proceeded to have her get up, yanked her chair away, and climbed under the table chasing that steak. It had rolled several feet and was almost still sizzling on the floor just at Beverly's feet.

He grabbed the steak with his bare hands, slammed it on Dolores's plate, and said, "There it is, now don't cry about it!"

The rest of us at the table were laughing so hard at maniac Jim and feeling so bad for Dolores. What we all had for prom night dinner became forgettable.

I don't think Jim and Dolores dated again after prom night 1958.

Popcorn

I was born in late 1940. As I remember, from the time I was four years old or so, every movie theater would have double feature, a newsreel, and a cartoon, sometimes two cartoons, which was always great for me. After dinner many times, my mom and dad would take us to a movie. Usually, we would arrive when the middle of the second feature was being shown. Then we would find three or four seats depending if my ten-years-older brother would come with us. After disrupting the moviegoers in the chosen row, we would sit down and try to figure out the plot of the movie that was showing. Actually, I wouldn't have understood it anyway. I was just waiting for the cartoon. Anyway, we would sit through the portion of the second feature, wait for the main attraction, watch that in full, then wait 'til the second feature got to "this is where we came in," then we would get up and leave. Usually, I would fall asleep long before that happened. If I saw the cartoon, I felt fulfilled for the evening. The point of this digression is to further illustrate how moviegoing has changed. As I remember, no one ever cared when a movie started; you just went to a movie. The first time I remember the starting time of a movie being important was for Alfred Hitchcock's *Psycho*. The movie ads said that no one would be seated during the last twenty minutes of the feature. How strange was that?

There was a new beautiful and quite large movie theater named Des Peres Cinema. (The movie theaters were used to be called "movie theaters," but now they are "cinemas." I guess that makes them sound much more fashionable.) This chapter is not intended to be a parenthetical chapter, but I feel that a digression would fit here . . . later to be assigned to its proper location. This new, beautiful, and quite large "cinema" was showing a new movie with Robert Redford called *The Great Waldo Pepper.* This was mid-1975 and it was the first time we had seen Susan Sarandon. She didn't last very long in the movie, but she made a positive impression. As usual, with our movie dates, Susan and I would enter the auditorium when all the lights were on and choose our seats, and then I would go to the lobby to get the popcorn and drinks (I would secretly add a box of Jujyfruits) and head back to our seats. For this particular showing, I got the popcorn and returned to our chosen location. The lights were still on, and I was holding this long tube-shaped tub of popcorn. For some reason that I have been unable to figure out, I felt the popcorn tub start slipping in my grasp. I squeezed it tighter to prevent losing it, but like a rocket launch, the popcorn box exploded from my hand, showering three or four rows with a cloudburst of popcorn. The rows of moviegoers were laughing uproariously. As a matter of fact, I think the whole theater was laughing, except Susan . . . she was pretending that she didn't know me. I was really embarrassed but laughing because I had no idea what large an area could be covered with one box of popcorn.

With a somewhat sheepish grin, I went back to the concession stand while holding my empty box that once contained popcorn. I said to the concession lady that I spilled my box of popcorn (resisting the urge to tell her how it exploded), and she very graciously took the box and filled it again for me.

As I entered the auditorium again with the box of popcorn, the lights were out and the movie started. I found our row and started apologizing for the disruption when once again I felt the popcorn slipping. Not wanting it to spill again, I increased the pressure of my grasp, and unbelievably, the popcorn container shot skyward and showered the three or four rows with another hail of popcorn.

From the back of the theater, I heard someone shout, "It's the *same guy!*"

Susan hung her head in disbelief.

I forgot about getting another box, and I think we both missed the first half hour or so of the movie because we were attempting to be invisible.

The World's Greatest Blackjack Dealer

I hadn't been to a casino for several years, but after Susan died, I brooded for several months and decided to see if I still remembered how to play blackjack. There is a casino in downtown St. Louis that is named Lumiere and is quite beautiful inside with lots of yellow and burnt orange walls and carpeting. It sort of reminds me of the old Wilbur Clark's Desert Inn, which was one of the few non-glitzy but very elegant casinos in Las Vegas. So I went to Lumiere as some sort of diversion. Standing behind a blackjack table was a very beautiful and stately red-haired lady whose table was empty, so I approached and sat down to try my luck. This dealer was very personable, incredibly accurate, and the perfect diversion for me. Her name was Marina and she spoke English very well. But being originally from Azerbaijan, which was part of the U.S.S.R., she spoke Russian as her native language. We seemed to have a sort of connection other than the blackjack table, and she seemed to like me as I definitely liked her.

To my mind, it seems to be that the last thing to occur in learning a new language is the subtlety of humor. This very beautiful Marina Melikova, the best and most attractive dealer I had ever experienced, seemed to possess a very fine sense of humor. We made each other laugh from time to time. I am a very firm believer that humor heals many wounds, and she got me laughing on many occasions and certainly assisted in healing several of my wounds. Also, I must tell you, I was very lucky playing at her table and won a nice sum on that first session. I was also very lucky playing at her table the second time when I went back the next day. Then the next day after that . . . and so on, and so on.

Marina quickly became a friend of mine, and I kept hoping that we could become more than just friends. However, there was one seemingly insurmountable issue. Marina was considerably younger than me, and I felt that I was just living in a dream world thinking that we could have a relationship beyond the table. After a couple of months, she asked me for my phone number.

I started to write it down for her, and she said, "No, you can't pass anything to me. Just tell me, and I'll remember it."

I told her my number and waited for her to call me. I waited, and waited, and waited some more. Then one evening after I was playing at her table that afternoon, she called. We talked for almost a half hour or so when I got the courage to ask her out to dinner. Astonishingly, she accepted my offer, and we met for lunch at Smokey Bones. We had a great time (at least I did), and it seemed to me there was a possibility for a deeper relationship beyond "hit me."

My adult son, Daniel, and I had made reservations at Disney World to spend Thanksgiving and celebrate my birthday, which fell on Thanksgiving, November 26. Marina and I spoke many times on Thanksgiving that year because she was cooking a duck for dinner. Every time we spoke during that afternoon, there were more problems cooking that duck . . . it just wasn't getting cooked completely. She tried many things in cooking that stupid duck and called me often asking for suggestions. I had none. Finally, as I recall, she just cut up the duck, fried the pieces, and made duck soup. We really established a relationship on those phone calls. I couldn't wait to see her again. I called her as soon as I got back to St. Louis, and we met for dinner at Outback.

After dinner, she said to me, "You know, if we see each other outside of the casino, you can never play at my table."

I realized that and told her that it was her call. She had to make the decision.

She paused for a short time, then said, "I don't want you to play at my table again."

I must explain how different we are in age, and I guess how I come by it naturally. My grandfather was born in 1836 and that is not a misprint. Not my great-great-grandfather, but my grandfather was born in 1836 and fought in the Civil War as a scout for (as he told my father) Robert E. Lee. He married my grandmother, and my father was born when his father was seventy-one and his mother was thirty-three. Their age difference was thirty-eight years. Marina is thirty-seven years younger than I am, but I guess if it's okay with her, then it is okay and very thrilling to me.

Marina and I have been together for almost ten years, and she is even more beautiful that she was when I played that first hand of blackjack at her table. I hired her for my company, Missouri Brick Company, and she is a spitfire of delight to our employees as well as our customers. Marina is easily the greatest thing that ever happened to me in my later years. She is gorgeous, and we have been living together, along with her mother (who is younger than me), her daughter named Ramina who is a junior in high school, two cats, and a dog named Bella who has a world-class insatiable appetite. Marina is indeed a pleasure to live with. However, now when I say "hit me," I have to duck.

YANKEE DOODLE DIXIE

In the early seventies, St. Louis began a very short-lived trend of bringing top names in the entertainment industry to appear in small venues such as barn dinner theaters, restaurants, and nightclubs. I say short-lived because it came and went so fast that it was almost over before it started. Barbara Streisand appeared at the Crystal Palace on Gaslight Square, and the Smothers Brothers also appeared at that venue. The Four Freshmen performed at the Ramada Inn, Patti Paige was at the Barn Dinner Theater, the World's Greatest Jazz Band was at the Chase Hotel, and Rich Little (my lookalike) was at the Cheshire Inn. Carlos Montoya (great guitarist) was at the United Hebrew Temple, and Andres Segovia (greater guitarist) performed at the Kiel Opera House. What a great period of time for entertainment in St. Louis. Just as a side story regarding the Segovia performance, the theater was packed, and Segovia walked on stage carrying his guitar, sat on a folding chair on stage, and started playing a Bach fugue. Less than a minute into his performance, someone in the audience coughed. Segovia stopped playing immediately and rested his guitar on his knee while someone else coughed, then another person, and then it seemed like the entire theater coughed. When there was total silence, Segovia continued playing that Bach fugue exactly where he left off.

Another performer during this great glut entertainment salvo was Chet Atkins, whose performance at the Barn Dinner Theater was absolutely remarkable. Chet's style was alone in its greatness at that time in the country guitar world. He used his thumb as base accompaniment to the other fingers on his right hand. It was almost like that thumb was a third hand that was totally independent of the other fingers on his hand. The further remarkable aspect of his playing was that in the most intense and exciting part of whatever he was playing, he appeared totally relaxed. I don't think he ever broke a sweat. The most incredible part of his performance was his playing of "Yankee Doodle Dixie" at the same time on the guitar, with his fingers playing Dixie while his thumb was playing Yankee Doodle. It seemed totally impossible, yet I saw him do it. We were in the second-row center, and I watched him carefully, and no digits became detached.

I made a living (sort of) in a vocal trio with two remarkable musicians, Lon Gilbert on guitar and Barry Oxenhandler on banjo and guitar. I also played guitar. I was actually a French horn and trumpet player, and barely adequate on the guitar. Susan, a very talented guitarist, gave me a beautiful Martin O-18 guitar for our fifth anniversary. It was far beyond my musical ability, but nonetheless a gorgeous musical instrument. The day after the Chet Atkins concert, I sat on the balcony of our apartment and attempted to play "Yankee Doodle Dixie" at the same time, just as Chet. A foolish attempt at best. I struggled for over three hours and finally got the opening phrase of Yankee Doodle with my thumb (Yankee Doodle went to town) and the opening phrase of Dixie (I wish I was in the land of cotton) with my fingers. I was incredibly proud of myself and called to Susan to hear it. I played it for her, and it actually sounded correct.

She said, "How did you do that?"

I said that I first started out playing Dixie with my fingers, and while I was playing that by note, I thought Yankee Doodle and worked it in with my thumb.

She said, "Good grief, Don, you could drive yourself crazy and tie your brain in a knot."

I replied, "You are right, baby, my head is tied in a knot at this very moment!"

Susan said that I shouldn't think of it as two different songs, that I should write it out and just play it as one piece. She took a piece of manuscript paper, wrote the two different melodies as one piece, she then took my guitar, and played it perfectly on the first try that took maybe twenty seconds.

I was so embarrassed. I got up and left the apartment without even saying goodbye. I don't recall talking to her at all for several days.

Three Quickies with Susan
(I Just Loved Quickies with Susan)

Susan and I were on a road trip traveling for a couple of hours when we saw a road sign advertising "Stuckey's next exit." We were both getting a little hungry, and maybe some good rural home cooking might just fill the bill. Stuckey's stores were small diners with huge stores that contained forgettable trinkets. I don't know if any still exist, but they had great pecans and home-cooked meals. We pulled onto the lot and entered the store. The diner was to the right, and all of the trinkets were to the left. We turned right, entered the dining section, and found an unoccupied booth. A "Flo-type" waitress came up and took our drink orders. Behind the counter of the restaurant, there was a menu describing all of the dining options. One of the options said "Friedham Sandwich." I thought, well, I guess that is some sort of country specialty until I realized that the letters were all scrunched together.

I asked Susan if she had ever heard of a "Freedom Sandwich" (carefully planting the mispronouncing in her mind), and she said, "No, I never have heard of a freedom sandwich. I'll ask the waitress." (*Aha* . . . I got her.) The waitress returned to take our order, and Susan said "Ma'am, what is a Freedom Sandwich?"

The waitress replied, "I don't know."

"What do you mean you don't know? It is on your menu board."

The waitress looked at the board and said, "Mah'em, that is a Fryhed Hahem."

Susan realized how I set her up and really laughed at her mistake. Another quickie . . . .

Susan was a very proper lady and even knew which side of the plate the knife and spoon went, as well as the napkin and fork. She was very well schooled in proper decorum. We were dining at a very trendy white tablecloth restaurant in the Central West End area of St. Louis named Balaban's. We placed our orders, and the salads were brought with a dressing cruet on the side. My salad had some large leafy lettuce that needed to be cut up somewhat. I took my knife and fork and started to cut when, I guess, the knife caught a large piece of lettuce, and my salad exploded all over the tablecloth. I knew Susan was looking at me, but I never looked nor even caught her eye. I very carefully took the salad dressing cruet and started dolloping the lettuce where it landed on the table. I was doing it very precisely, not spilling any of the dressing on the tablecloth, just dripping it perfectly on each piece of lettuce on the table and never looking at Susan. I knew she was embarrassed but loving it.

I heard her saying while laughing, "Oh *no*."

The third little quickie . . . .

Susan loved a chocolatier in St. Louis named Bissinger's Handcrafted Chocolatier. In Susan's words, their raspberry creams were "to die for." Susan's birthday was April 13. So for her birthday one year, I gave her a two-pound box of those overly sweet confections. It became a nightly ritual that around 9:30 p.m., I would bring her the box, and she would remove three or four of the chocolates, not removing the little paper wrappers holding them. Every night, she would rummage through the empty wrappers seeking a few more chocolates, never removing the wrappers from the box. When it was obvious to me, but not to Susan, that the chocolates were getting fewer and fewer, I returned to Bissinger's and bought another box. I secretly added a few chocolates to the original box, and Susan kept exhibiting great joy when she discovered a few more left. Eventually, the new box needed replacing, so I went back to Bissinger's and told them the story about the nightly hunt. I bought another one-pound box, and they thought it was so funny, so they gave me another box for free. I continued secretly reloading the original box until that two-pound box became over ten pounds of chocolates . . . with Susan never noticing. Every night, she would forage and get thrilled finding a few more. Finally, after running out of finances to satisfy her raspberry cream addiction, I had to tell her what I had done.

She laughed with that ever so delightful way of hers and said, "Well, I guess I was the perfect victim of your loveable prank. You are free to do that again whenever you wish."

THE GREAT GIPPO

I have been very fortunate in my life to have had many friends. Most of them were very intelligent and talented. A very select few stand out as being extraordinarily talented. The "Great Gippo" is one of them. Jan Gippo was the piccoloist (piccolo picker) for the St. Louis Symphony for thirty-five years or so. I once introduced Jan (pronounced "Yahn") to a friend of mine and described him as one of the top two piccoloists in the world.

Jan, being ever so humble, said, "No, I am probably one of the top three. Rampal and Galway are very good flutists and play the piccolo also. I must be behind them."

That is Jan, always deferring to other greats of the world. Jan commissioned the highly respected composer, Lowell Lieberman, to compose a piccolo concerto for him. When Lowell Lieberman completed the composition, Jan performed the world premier of that concerto at the National Flute Convention in New York City, with the orchestral ensemble being members of the New Jersey Symphony.

I am always using silly accents when I call Jan on the phone and always get him laughing.

One early Sunday morning, Jan was awakened by a phone call from a man with a very strong Irish accent who said, "Good morning, Mr. Gippo."

Jan said, "Marquess, that is the worst Irish accent I have ever heard."

The caller was James Galway, the premier flute player in the world who was born in Belfast, Ireland, and was blessed with a beautiful Irish brogue. Jan apologized to James and said he thought it was a friend pulling a prank. Jan embarrassedly called me later and told me about his blunder. James Galway wanted permission from Jan to record the Lieberman composition.

Later that morning, when I was certain that Jan was at his Sunday morning radio broadcast *From the Garden Live*, I called his number, got his voicemail, and said in a French accent, "Oh ho ho, Monsieur Gippo, do not let that Irishman record your concerto. Theese ees Jean Pierre Rampal. I must have eet for myself to record."

Later that evening, the phone rang at home. Susan answered it in the kitchen, and I could hear her laughing.

She then called out to me from the kitchen: "Oh, Jean Pierre, Monsieur Gippo wants to speak with you!"

As mentioned earlier, Jan Gippo was incredibly brilliant and an extremely talented musician. But like all gifted individuals, he was somewhat absentminded and a little confused from time to time. This next story is one of those instances where a "you would have to be there" statement would apply. Nevertheless, I will make an attempt to describe it. We were in the car together. He was driving, and we were passing by Washington University. I asked him if he would be available for a poker game Saturday night at my house.

He said, "I don't know. I will have to check with Allen."

I said, "Who is Allen?"

He said, "I didn't mean Allen, I meant Carl."

I said, "Who is Carl?"

He responded, "Jane Allen is a terrific piano instructor. Jane Carl is the lady I am almost engaged to. How I got that so confused with both of their first names being Jane is very confusing to me. If I could have a picture of my brain at that moment, it would be quite a blur. Where that came from, I don't know."

I responded, "Third base." (For those of you that understand that remark, no explanation is needed. For those that don't understand it, an explanation is impossible.)

Jan, who is a little over six feet tall and at the time several thousand pounds overweight, gave a concert at the Royal Academy of Music in London, which was a great success.

The next day, the writer of his rave review started the review by saying, "Jan Gippo, a very large man with a very small instrument . . . ."

One of my favorite writers is Max Shulman (*Many Loves of Dobie Gillis, Rally Round the Flag Boys*, etc.), who had a character named Crip in one of his books (I think it was *Sleep to Noon*) who was so named because he always had a broken limb, a sprained ankle, or some other ailment in that he was always on crutches or had some part of his body in a cast. Jan, who was always very healthy, developed a series of physical problems late in his life that greatly reminded me of Shulman's Crip. Jan, who was an insulin-dependent diabetic (he had a stomach stapling for weight control) told me that he was diagnosed with a fatty liver that is similar to cirrhosis but not alcohol-induced. It was cancerous and he needed a new liver. But before that could be accomplished, the doctor detected some heart issue that needed to be taken care of, which required several hospital stays. Something in that operation required additional surgery, and it seemed to me that almost weekly there was some other domino falling that required something else, after something else, after something else. Finally, all was clear for a new liver for Jan. The operation was a success. His old liver was removed and a new liver was installed. Happy Day! Jan is of Norwegian Jewish ethnicity, and like much of the Jewish population, he possesses a great sense of humor, so I felt that my homecoming gift from the hospital for him would be accepted with the proper spirit. After I determined that he was going to continue to live and everything worked out well, as a gift for his arrival home, I contacted a Jewish deli and ordered a chopped liver on rye with a little onion and Gulden's mustard.

The owner of the deli, whose name was Saul, after being told what I wanted to do and why, said, "Ooh, I have got to be a part of this!" He couldn't stop laughing.

I requested that Saul would have a note inserted for the delivery with the chopped liver on rye that stated, "Welcome home . . . . I don't know where this liver came from, but I have my suspicions! From your friend and mine, Don."

Michael Barnes and The Seventieth Home-Run Ball

I had achieved a degree of success with my baseball art photos. I read in the paper the day after Phil Ozersky, a scientist at Washington University Medical School, caught Mark McGwire's seventieth home-run baseball and he hadn't decided what to do with it. I found his name in the phone book (remember those?), called him and left a message saying that I had an idea that could be profitable for him, and he could still retain the ball and decide what to do with it later. I would just need the ball for a few minutes. At that time, I had an exhibit of my photos at the Cardinals Hall of Fame and had achieved a certain degree of credibility. I left my phone number and hoped that he would call me back. He didn't . . . but his attorney, Michael Barnes, who was handling the merchandising of Phil Ozersky's good fortune, left a message that I should call him with my proposal. At this moment, I hadn't totally formulated what my proposal was, but I felt that I should call him back and tell him what I planned to do, and how much money he, Phil Ozersky, and I could make from my (yet to be determined) proposal. I formulated what I felt was a great idea for all parties and went over and over it in my mind in the hope that he would agree and we could have the contract produced. I was very nervous about the entire situation because I knew that it could be a career-enhancing move. I kept rehearsing my call over and over in my head and finally had everything straight for my idea and had the courage to pick up the phone to call Michael Barnes.

I called, and his phone call was answered with his message: "Thanks for calling Michael Barnes, sports attorney. Leave a message, and I will return your call as soon as possible."

I said very strongly (this was really important to me) in my rich radio voice, "Hi, this is Michael Barnes . . . . No, wait a minute, you are Michael Barnes, and I am . . . . Well, it no longer matters who I am . . . . Goodbye." I blew it.

I called again the next day, and Michael himself answered. I told him who I was and that my proposition was as follows: I would photograph Mark McGwire's seventieth home-run ball, produce seventy signed and numbered Cibachrome thirty-by-forty-inch prints selling for $2,500 each with $500 donated to Cardinals Care, and the remaining $2,000 to be split equally between Phil Ozersky and the Marquess Gallery. Also, I would produce a total of seven thousand eighteen-by-twenty-four-inch special prints selling for $70 each, with $10 of each print donated to Cardinals Care and the remaining $60 to be split equally between Phil Ozersky and the Marquess Gallery. Michael Barnes thought it was a terrific idea and said that I should have my attorney draw up the agreement. The eighteen-page document was produced and signed by both parties. As a postscript, Phil Ozersky auctioned the ball at Guernsey's in New York, and Todd McFarlane (the cartoonist of *Spawn*) was the successful bidder at $3.14 million dollars. Barry Bonds, several years later, greatly devalued that investment when he hit seventy-three home runs.

LAS VEGAS
(WE'RE GONNA KILL 'EM)

A very good friend of mine years ago was a man named Lon Gilbert. Lon was a very fine guitarist and had an incredibly rich baritone voice. Lon, Barry Oxenhandler, Susie Drozda, and I sang in what I considered at the time to be an excellent folk quartet that was destined for greatness. Our group achieved marginal success for a while, then split up, and went our individual ways. Lon loved to gamble, however for the most part, that love was unrequited. Lon was skillful, however very unlucky. I have always considered myself luckier than skillful when it comes to gambling, which is a situation that most gamblers prefer.

Lon Gilbert married a very beautiful and statuesque lady named Donna Daugherty, who could have very easily been a top model. They were getting married on a Saturday in early April, and he wanted to spend their honeymoon weekend in Las Vegas. He invited Susan and I to come along, and I was just fine with that. Lon had never been to Las Vegas, but I had been there several times and just loved it. They got married, and the next weekend we were going to Vegas. Sadly, in the middle of the week, Donna got the flu and just couldn't travel. Without Donna, Susan decided that she wouldn't go either, so Lon and I went to Las Vegas anyway to celebrate his honeymoon. Very strange indeed, but the trip to Vegas excited both of us enough that we were going anyway . . . without the girls!

It was to be a very short trip, leaving Friday morning and returning Sunday night. As we were on the plane, Lon asked me how much money I was bringing, so I told him that I was taking just a little over $400. He said that was strange, as it was the same amount that he was taking. This was 1970, and that truly seemed to be a considerable amount to take for just a weekend.

Lon then stated, "We are going to kill 'em." Of course.

The plane touched down at 10 a.m., and we got to the very long taxi line and finally got into a cab. Lon asked the driver where the cheapest hotels are in Las Vegas, and the cabbie told him that they were downtown, definitely not on the strip.

Lon said, "Great, take us downtown."

I hadn't spent much time downtown, as the several times I had been there, I stayed on the strip. The hotels downtown that I remember at the time were the Fremont, the Mint, the Four Queens, the Las Vegas Club, and the brand-new Union Plaza Hotel. All of the hotels had signs in the windows advertising their breakfast specials, which you won't believe: two eggs, hash browns, bacon, toast, and coffee for thirty-nine cents. It is true, you can look it up (Casey Stengel). We checked in to the cheapest hotel we could find (we didn't want to waste any of our gambling money), which was the Las Vegas Club Hotel. It cost $18.75 per night, which included two free breakfasts. What a deal! We got to the room that had two twin beds (thank goodness), a shower only, and in the upper right corner of the room there was a black-and-white TV chained and secured with a padlock. I had no idea that anything like this existed in Las Vegas. There was also a McDonald's restaurant downtown, which we frequented several times.

So we went across the street to the brand-new Union Plaza Hotel to take all their money. This was around two o'clock in the afternoon. We still had our $400 each. We hadn't lost a dime. I found a $5 blackjack table and proceeded on my quest for untold fortune. After about an hour or so, I had taken the casino for $35 and was a very happy player. Lon came up to me and asked to borrow some money. An hour plus at the tables and he blew his entire $400 or so. I loaned him my $35 winnings, and he went away, only to return a half hour or so later, broke again. I was very lucky again and loaned him my latest $40 winnings. Therefore, a pattern was set. Once I loaned it to Lon, I couldn't lose it, so I inadvertently opened up a savings account in Las Vegas. I wasn't continually a winner, but I was doing much better than Lon. Remember, we had only been there a couple of hours and had a full couple of days ahead. In Las Vegas, if you are playing at a table, the drinks are free. Lon would sit at a table, order a "free" drink, and before it got delivered, he would lose another $15–$20.

I told him that it would be much cheaper to just go to the bar and order his gin and tonic, but he said, "Hey, they are free at the tables."

The weekend progressed with roughly the same pattern. I had only about $250 of my $400 left, but Lon owed me about $450, so it was a profitable trip for me. We played and played until it was crunch time for the plane's departure. We caught a cab to the airport. Lon had no money to pay half, so I paid the entire cab bill. We then got to the airport and literally ran to the gate just in time to make the plane. When we got back to St. Louis, we couldn't have gotten my car off the lot were it not for me. Lon is a very intelligent individual with a *bachelor's* degree, but somehow or another, he leaves that intelligence elsewhere when he enters a gambling venue.

His honeymoon was very enjoyable for me, especially, and I enjoyed depositing the $485 check he wrote to me. Viva Las Vegas!

KENNENBUNKPORT, MAINE

Susan, before we were married, worked for BOAC (British Overseas Airline Company) in Denver, Colorado, as a travel agent booking flights and trips worldwide. Susan was born in New Jersey and traveled throughout New England, a location that she felt needed to be photographed by me. She used her extensive travel agent abilities to book our New England trip. She booked spectacular bed-and-breakfast inns for the four of us—Susan, Danny, Donny, and me—and the trip was perfect. We went to see Niagara Falls and stayed at the Asa Ransom House in Clarence, New York, where the room was terrific and the food was spectacular. We visited Boston and enjoyed Durgin Park with the surly waitresses and the terrific food. The New England Aquarium was worth the entire trip alone, and we were having a wonderful time indeed. We stayed at the Ramada Inn that was owned by a friend's cousin, and the accommodations were comfortable indeed. As I remember, the hotel was on Soldiers Memorial Parkway just off Storrow Drive. The drive to the New England Aquarium was a short forty-minute drive from the hotel.

We got lost heading back to our hotel from the aquarium driving on Storrow Drive when for the first ten miles there were signs saying "Storrow Drive Left" or "Storrow Drive Right." Then we came to a fork in the road with no mention of Storrow Drive at all. Apparently, we chose the wrong tine of that fork because Storrow Drive was mentioned no more. Being a typical guy who never asks for directions, I drove on for about another half hour or so (it only took us forty minutes to get from Ramada Inn on Soldiers Memorial Drive to the New England Aquarium, but so far we had been traveling back two hours or so trying to find it). Susan finally convinced me to stop and ask for directions . . . definitely a nonmacho thing for a man of my stature. Guys just don't stop to ask for directions. There was a gas station ahead, so I pulled over, went inside, and asked the attendant how to find the Ramada Inn on Soldiers Memorial Drive. As he was giving me directions, another customer came in, interrupted the clerk, and asked me what we were looking for. I told him where we were headed, and the clerk continued giving me directions.

The customer looked at the clerk and said to him, "What kind of idiot are you? They will never get there that way."

The clerk said, "Who are you calling an idiot? I know this is the best way for them to find it."

The customer yelled at the clerk and used several imaginative couplings of four-letter words. The clerk yelled back at him, and, fearing that it might come to blows, I left, went to the car, and started heading in the general direction that both of them seemed to agree upon. When I got to the car and told Susan what had happened in the filling station, she wasn't surprised at all.

She said that, "Helpful Bostonians are like that."

An hour or so later, we saw the red neon sign that said Ramada and hoped it was the one that had our clothing in the room. Lucky us, it was.

Our next stop was the Ralph Waldo Emerson Inn in Rockport, Maine, which was situated on the beach of the Atlantic Ocean and had a great restaurant that had terrific food and a great view of the sea. So far, Susan had mapped out the perfect trip for us. We then proceeded north to Kennebunkport, which was a very scenic ocean "fishing village" for, I guess, the super wealthy.

Kennebunkport was extremely picturesque, and Susan booked a room for us at the Kennebunkport Inn, which was a converted several-hundred-year-old mansion. It couldn't have been more beautiful (nor more expensive) and, as I recall, sat at the top of a hill overlooking the quaint shops of the port. One of the major attractions of Kennebunkport was a point on the sea a couple miles north of the village, where Spouting Rock and Blowing Cave were located. Susan and the boys wanted to spend time at the beach, so I armed myself with my three cameras and headed to the point on the rocks where I could make "great art." I reached the point and there was a small sign that said, No Climbing on the Rocks. The sign was small, and I figured, what the hell, great art lies ahead. I was the only person anywhere around and felt I could be wherever I wanted. I climbed out onto the rocks, and there was an opening in the rocks where a pool of ocean water was located. I started using my cameras to photograph whatever I thought would make interesting "art." From out of nowhere, two guys in stocking caps and turtleneck sweaters stood next to me on the rocks overlooking spouting rock. I was a little frightened, but they asked me for my identification and wanted to know just what in the hell I was doing there. I showed them my driver's license as well as my photography business card. They frisked me and treated me like a criminal suspect. I asked them what was going on, and they pointed out a beautiful home right across the inlet. There was a flag raised, and they said that that meant that the vice president, George H. W. Bush, was in residence. His summer home was on Walker Point, which was just across the inlet. After convincing them that I was just a guy taking pictures, they left me alone on the rocks. They were Secret Service men protecting the vice president of the United States. Apparently, I convinced them that I was harmless and no threat to the veepee, so they went away and left me alone on the rocks. Anyway, after they left, I stood on the rocks with cameras in hand ready to take some magnificent photos. It was an overcast day and the light was somewhat gloomy, but I was there anyway ready to make the perfect photograph. I looked down at the pool of water surrounded by these massive rocks, and the water came in and made a little "bloop."

The water spouted about six inches several times, and I thought, "Well this is a tiny area away from most entertainment, and the people here must be starved for any small bit of excitement they can find."

I started shooting when I heard a giant "*roar.*" Aha, I thought, "Blowing cave!" Loud roar, probably greater than most ocean roars, but no big deal. As I was waiting for the next little "bloop," another intense roar occurred and the spouting rock spouted! A geyser exploded and spewed water probably six feet above me through the rocks. I was almost washed off the rocks and into the sea. I was soaked, and my cameras were soaking wet. I guess the fact that I was in danger and about to be going to Davy Jones' Locker didn't concern the Secret Service guys. As long as I had no high-powered rifle, I was on my own.

I made it back to my car and headed to the beach to spend some quality time with Susan and the boys.

Susan asked if I had gotten some great shots, and I said, "I'll tell you later!"

I spent two days later on a deep-sea fishing boat, which was a great thrill as well as being very productive. I must have caught ten or more large cod and had a whole lot of fun doing so.

After Kennebunkport, we headed north for Bar Harbor (pronounced Bah Habah), where Susan had not booked any place for us and we were just going to wing it. Winging it never took flight because everything was booked, so we went inland and spent the night in Bangor, Maine. With no further excitement in Bangor, nor Bah Habah, we started the long drive home.

JOHN CURRY MARQUESS

My father was Robert Lee Marquess, named after Robert E. Lee, the great Confederate general. The reason? My father's father fought in the Civil War. If you do the math, that seems impossible; however, here is the explanation: My father was born in 1907 when his father was seventy-one years of age. My grandfather, John Curry Marquess, was born in 1836 and fought for the South in the Civil War. (I have the muzzle-loading rifle that he carried.) As my father told me, his father was a scout for Lee. This is not known to be a provable fact, however, that is what my grandfather told my father. Upon further conversations with Civil War historians, he was probably a spy for the South, whether directly reporting to Lee or not. The reason for that statement is that he told my father that most of the time, he did not wear his uniform when he went beyond enemy lines, and that determined that he was a spy. My dad told me many stories of his father hiding out in barns and keeping himself warm under hay. My dad also expressed disbelief that many nights his father kept from freezing by covering himself with leaves and piling snow on top of the leaves.

My grandfather survived the war and purchased one thousand acres of tobacco land in western Kentucky in a teeny-tiny town named Pee Dee. From what my father told me, he probably owned the town. He was the largest taxpayer in Christian County, Kentucky. When his first wife died, he became a very desirable widower. Trying to do the extrapolation from what my father told me, as well as researched records, my grandmother was thirty-three years old when my father was born. The first child from their marriage was stillborn, and my father was their second child. My grandfather's first marriage was childless. My grandmother, Frances Redd, was twenty-nine years of age, and my grandfather was sixty-eight when they married.

I have a letter written in beautiful script in February 1861 by my grandfather to his brother, James Marquess, stating that there definitely would be a war. The US government, so my grandfather felt, lied to the South and ignored the Mason–Dixon Line agreement in considering to allow California to enter the Union as a free state. Per the Mason–Dixon agreement, all states above this imaginary line would be free states and those below would be slave states. The state of California spanned that line and wanted to enter as a free state. My grandfather felt that the South would not allow this without a fight. Therefore, war was inevitable. The South was greatly dependent on slave labor for the production of cotton.

Furthermore, you hear stories of the Civil War in which brother fought brother. My grandfather's brother, James Marquess, who lived in Ohio and fought for the North, was captured by the South. My grandfather interceded and got his brother released, but James had to sign a document to "fight no more." In my family, brother really did fight brother.

Another interesting part of my heritage is that my sixth-generational grandfather was a pirate who was hanged for treason. John Curry Marquess was the son of William Kidd Marquess II. William Kidd Marquess II was the grandson of William Kidd Marquess, who was the grandson of Captain William Kidd (1655–1701), the pirate (privateer, according to my family) who was hanged for treason at the age of forty-seven. The lineage is directly to me in that he is my great-great-great-great-great-great-grandfather. My brother, Robert K. Marquess, my father's cousin, Wes Marquess, and my wife, Susan, all researched the history of William Kidd and came up with identical results.

I truly don't know if this has any connection whatsoever, but I have never been seasick in my life. I have been on a small boat with four sailors in the Pacific Ocean when a vicious storm attacked and all four sailors got extremely sick, but not me. I was on a cruise ship when the stabilizers stopped working and 90 percent of the passengers were greatly ill, but not me. I am not fully aware of whether my ancestry has anything to do with that, but it is a curiosity.

Hotel Colombi

In the Missouri brick business, we represented the largest manufacturer of split tile in the world named Gail Tile, which was located in Giessen, West Germany. We were very successful in securing sales for that company, and I was invited to their factory on many occasions. Gail had developed an incredibly strong ceramic that was only one-eight-inch thick but could be extruded seamlessly for twenty feet or more. I was invited to the plant to view this new and very innovative product.

The USA representative and very close friend, Bill Haslett, was there for the unveiling, and Bill and I were offered a new Opel station wagon to use for a week to tour Europe. This was an incredible opportunity for us. Bill and I purchased a new Michelin Guide and mapped our trip. Since Bill was a gourmet and I loved to eat, we carefully mapped our trip based on the number of toques (chef hats) shown after each restaurant review. We had a culinary experience awaiting.

Our first stop was Rothenburg ob de Tauber, which was a walled city untouched by World War II bombings. The Isenhut (White House) was our first stop for a hotel and dining. I took care of the room negotiations since we were looking for a deal for two rooms. Since it was off-season, we got a very good rate for both rooms. The dinner was spectacular, and the tour of the tenth-century village was great. We both walked the wall.

The next stop was Brussels, Belgium, where the waffles were absolutely the very best in the world. We traveled south from there to Luxembourg, where the capital of Luxembourg is Luxembourg, and stayed in a terrific very old hotel and dinned at a gourmet "Chinese" restaurant.

The next morning, leaving Luxembourg, the fog was so thick that the sides of the Autobahn were invisible. I was driving and felt very nervous traveling when it was difficult to see fifty feet ahead. I was driving at eighty kilometers (forty-eight miles per hour), and cars were flying past us at very high speeds. I guessed that they were used to driving blind. When we reached the border of France, all traffic slowed to a crawl. A gendarme stopped us, and I asked what happened.

He stated, "Two hundred car crash, four dead."

The highway closed, so we took an alternate route past Cherbourg to our destination, the Colombi Hotel in Freiburg. The hotel was one of the top hotels in Germany, and the restaurant showed five chef hats. It was our top dining adventure of the trip. We both ordered the chef's selection, which was a terrific meal including dessert for the costly price of $125 for each of us. Bill ordered a bottle of wine, which the waiter placed in an ice bucket behind Bill's chair. Dining at a table next to us were a very elegant appearing couple celebrating something. The man had snow-white hair and resembled Spencer Tracey in his later years. The lady was beautifully dressed in a very formal light orange gown.

As we were still dining, the waiter filled Bill's wine glass for the fourth time or so and emptied his bottle. Unknown to Bill, the waiter poured two glasses of wine for the couple next to us and then placed their bottle in the ice bucket behind Bill. Bill finished his last glass of wine and looked for the waiter to fill it. The waiter was nowhere around, so Bill just got up, went to the ice bucket, picked up the bottle, filled his glass, then placed the bottle back in the bucket, not seeing the glare of Spencer Tracey watching Bill, the ugly American, stealing his wine.

Bill sat down, took a sip, and with a very wild look in his eyes, said, "Ooh . . . that's really good!"

I saw the entire thing develop and just waited to see what would happen. I told Bill what he just did, and he looked over at the now-steaming man at the table next to us. Bill got up, walked over, and apologized to the man, who fortunately spoke English, and the man laughed and graciously accepted the apology. Our waiter came to the table, and Bill explained what happened and requested that our waiter offer the man a cigar from the cigar case. He did, and Spencer lookalike smiled and accepted the offering. The bill came for us, and Bill said that that was the first time he has ever seen a cigar that cost fifty-two dollars.

Henry Mancini, The Gentleman

One of the most beautiful shopping areas in the United States is the Country Club Plaza in Kansas City, Missouri. The architecture of the buildings is of Spanish influence developed by the J. C. Nichols Company after J. C. Nichols returned from a visit to Seville, Spain, in 1920. The shopping area is the first designed with the concept of autotransported customers. It consists of eighteen separate buildings comprising of over eight hundred thousand square feet of shopping area. It contains several boutique hotels and a very large and beautifully designed hotel originally named Alameda Plaza Hotel (now the Intercontinental Hotel) that was designed by architect Ward Haylett. Ward told me that the budget for the hotel was almost unlimited when he designed it for its opening in 1972. He told me that it was where "God would stay . . . if he could afford it."

I had a trip to Kansas City in 1981 several years after it opened, and Ward Haylett arranged for me to have a very beautiful suite that even had a grand piano in the room. It was terrific, needless to say. I had lusted for years for a Hart Schaffner Marx, Christian Dior three-piece suit, which I finally purchased for my visit. The suit was of a deep teal blue color and made of some sort of luxuriously soft cotton, and I felt very important wearing it. I considered myself very hot stuff.

On my day of checking in as I was walking through the lobby, Henry Mancini came walking toward me. Music has always been a very large part of my life, and Henry Mancini's compositions and arrangements were included in my short list of fabulous musical creations. His music for Peter Gunn and his music created for the movie *Hatari!* remain among my favorites even to this day. Henry's music for all of the *Pink Panther* movies for Blake Edwards is timeless. His compositions for many movies resulted in many Grammys, and his collaborations with the lyricist, Johnny Mercer, became some of the most popular musical compositions in history. My friend, Jan Gippo, who was with the St. Louis Symphony for over thirty-five years, told me that in a conversation with Henry Mancini, Henry told him that the royalties from "Moon River," paid for everything—his house, his cars, the education of his children, just everything. All other revenues were just "gravy."

As a related side story to this side story, my friend, Jan Gippo, the (almost) world's greatest piccoloist who related this story, was in the orchestra for a pops concert that Henry Mancini was guest-conducting. The "Star-Spangled Banner" march was on the program, and the very famous piccolo countermelody was ready to be performed with Jan Gippo standing and preparing to play when Henry Mancini asked to use Jan's piccolo and played it perfectly, probably not quite as well as the (almost) world's greatest piccoloist but nevertheless flawlessly. Jan told me that that proved to him that Henry Mancini was not only an incredible composer and arranger, but also a fine musician. He thanked Jan for the use of his piccolo and then returned to the conductor's podium.

At any rate, when I saw Henry Mancini heading toward me, I momentarily lost my scruples and said, "Hi, Hank, it's been a long time. Good to see you again!"

He stopped and said, "It has been, hasn't it . . . how have you been?" (My outright lie just went past him, and he was such a gentleman that he didn't confront me with "Who the hell are you?")

We stood and talked for maybe ten minutes, and he invited me to the Starlight Theater for his performance with the Kansas City

Philharmonic Orchestra. Sadly, I had to decline due to a business meeting that I had that evening.

But then he said, "Good seeing you again. Keep in touch."

I said, "Hank, you do the same."

I will always carry that guilt with me, but he was so cordial and considerate as well as very respectful toward me that I will also always carry that wonderful moment with me.

I will also wonder who he thought I was.

THE FABLED WATERS OF
THE SEA OF CORTEZ

Jim Sullivan, who was the president of Gail Tile, USA, put together a group of Gail distributors, who happened to be the top sales companies for Gail, and called it the "board of directors." It was actually the board of directors of nothing, it just had a neat sounding name. Once a year, Gail would host some lavish meeting of "the board," and in 1982, it was to be in a brand-new resort named "Los Arenas" on the tip of the Baja in Mexico at the mouth of the Sea of Cortez. I received the invitation letter and jumped at the opportunity.

The itinerary was to fly into Los Angeles and spend the night at Jim Sullivan's yacht club, the Balboa Bay Club, then travel to La Paz, Mexico, which was located on the Sea of Cortez side of the Baja, and then take a private plane down to the tip of the Baja to Los Arenas for three days and four nights of delicious food and fishing. The Balboa Bay Club was super posh, and Jim's new forty-five-foot cabin sailboat with sleeping berths below was dwarfed by the other craft at the club. Jim Sullivan was a sailor, as were the other two of the three of his guests. Phil Stalcup from Seattle had his own sailboat, as did Harry Atherton from Boston. Three of the four of us were seasoned sailors. Harry, Jim, and Phil had their fishing gear in PVC tubes to be carried on the plane with us to Los Arenas. These guys were serious deep-sea fishermen. Our plane for La Paz was leaving late in the afternoon, so we had time for a morning sail in Jim's brand-new sailboat. It was great fun especially for me since I had no experience and basically nothing to do, so I could just sit and relax and enjoy the beautiful morning's sail. The three other guys were doing what sailors do when sailing, which seems to be a lot. After the morning's sail, a wind came up as we approached the harbor returning Jim's sailboat to its slip. Jim thought that with three sailors on board, sailing the harbor sounded like it would work. Well . . . it didn't. With all of the jibbing and rigging and such, the wind was so strong that we collided with another sailboat that was leaving the harbor. Jim and the other two sailors thought that it was much funnier than the collided boat owner did, but apologies were made and there were no adverse consequences.

We then boarded the plane for our flight to La Paz, where we were taken to a private airstrip and a very small plane awaited our arrival. There was a pilot, but no copilot, so I occupied that seat. The pilot spoke no English, but he knew where we were headed (I hoped). The instrument readings were covered in dust and the pilot kept wiping them clean with a very dusty rag, and I thought that this flight might not make it to Los Arenas. After a while, a dirt runway appeared, and we landed and were taken to the resort by some sort of jeeplike vehicle. The resort was indeed very picturesque and brand-spanking-new. However, apparently the owner ran out of money when it came time to hire a cook and must have just found someone hiding behind a cactus and said, "Can you cook?," and hired him. The dining at the resort was a cut below Taco Bell. Sadly, it was the same with our fishing vessel. It was a twenty-two-foot boat with one outboard motor and one captain named Manuel.

We arrived at the beach at dawn where the boat was in the sand, with Manuel standing in the back. There were slots in front of the seats to rest the fishing poles, but not much of anything else . . . no seat belts. The four of us got on the boat, and my fishing pole was there for me. The other guys brought their poles (PVC pipes, remember). I never had much of a chance to deep-sea fish, but I was very open to the adventure. Our knowledgeable captain, Manuel, knew just where to go for us to catch "bait." At one point, all four of us had a fish on the line. We were catching bonita, which I understand to be of the tuna variety, however much smaller. The biggest fish I caught, Manuel cut up for bait. After an hour or so, we had enough bait, so Manuel hauled anchor and we headed further out to sea.

I considered it a very unfair competition, but we all put $10 in a "big fish pool." Those guys were taking advantage of me, but I really didn't care. This was fun, and I was loving it. Manuel prepared my line with bait, and we all dropped our lines hoping to lure a big one. We all caught several fish, and at the next location where we dropped our lines, I felt my line grow taut and thought that I had caught my hook on a rock or something. I leaned forward and wound the line tight again and kept repeating that for twenty to thirty minutes. This was no rock that I snagged.

As I kept reeling it in, Manuel shouted, "Rojo, rojo." Then I saw the bright reddish orange scales surface. I continued reeling him in, and Manuel screamed, "Rojo rojo," then pointed to me, flexed his arms, and called me "El Magnifico."

It was a 45½ pound red snapper. That was the biggest one he had ever seen. I was so proud of that fish that I carried it through the dining room of the resort and proudly showed it the diners. "Yep, I caught this fish all by myself. Isn't it gorgeous?"

I had heard many horror stories about the outrageous costs of stuffing a caught fish (fish taxidermists, I assume) and sending it back home. I thought the best thing to do with that red snapper was to eat it at the resort.

One of our group, Phil Stalcup, said, "I am not going to let their cook screw up this fish." So he filleted it and sautéed it with lemon, garlic, and butter. To this day, it was the best fish I have ever tasted in my life. After dinner, as I collected my $30 reward for the big fish pool, I reminded the guys of my newly dubbed title: "El Magnifico." Unfortunately, they voted and came up with another name far too fierce to mention.

The next morning, same routine, same bait catching, and then moving on to catch the big ones. Another "big fish" pool. I won it again with a sizable catch, not as large as big red but impressive anyway. That night, after collecting the big fish pool once again, I reminded them of my "El Magnifico" title. They voted and came up with that same insulting name from the night before.

The third day, we had no "beeg feesh" pool. Nevertheless, I caught the biggest fish. Then also, this third day, we went around the tip of the Baja and ventured far from shore into the Pacific Ocean. Toward the end of the day, a storm came up, and I was certain we were goners. Ninety percent of the time heading back to shore, the waves were so choppy that the propeller of the outboard motor was out of the water. (As one saving grace in our time of great peril, I thought that it would be a great legacy for my descendants to speak of me as perishing at the mouth of the Sea of Cortez in a deep-sea fishing boat . . . that certainly sounds more macho than getting crushed by a Good Humor truck while crossing Big Bend Boulevard, doesn't it?) The three sailors on our little fishing boat got very sick; however, I didn't.

I guess the nomenclature "El Magnifico" was very apt. (Tastefully, I neglected to remind my companions of such. But then again, those guys had been guzzling beer all day, and I guess they would have been just as sick in a much calmer sea.)

The last morning, we were driven to the dirt landing strip.

After waiting for forty-five minutes, a large Jeep vehicle met us, and the driver said, "Sometimes, the plane, she make it, and sometimes she doesn't."

This time she didn't. We jeeped back north to La Paz.

We made it back to La Paz, and our linguist (?), Jim Sullivan, explained to the cabbie at the hotel that he had heard about a saloon in La Paz that had a forty-foot bar that was made out of sterling silver and the bar stools were sterling silver saddles. It appeared that the driver understood, so we left the hotel and loaded in his cab. As we were driving, the bright lights of downtown La Paz faded in the distance. We were leaving the city. From Jim's description, the bar sounded like it was in the heart (maybe the pancreas) of activity of downtown La Paz. But then again, we really didn't know much at all regarding the nightlife in La Paz. Jim Sullivan was the only one of us who heard of this saloon, so trustfully we waited. Well, at this time, the bright lights of La Paz were so far behind us that they appeared as very foggy yellow mist in the rear-view mirror. We were definitely in the boonies of the Baja. Burning smudge pots appeared in the road ahead of us, but the driver didn't break speed. He just continued on the shoulder of the road and continued less than a half mile ahead, and an even more primitive dirt road was on the right. The cabbie made an abrupt right and continued his speed with the dust almost obliterating our view of anything. Shortly ahead, there was a parked large truck with a canvas top open in the back and four armed federales sitting in wait. We were entering a compound of some sort.

Mentally, it crossed my mind that the ransom note to the US government would say, "We got 'em, you want 'em? Send eighteen billion U.S. to La Paz, and you can have 'em back!" (A pipe dream of grandeur, to be sure. The figure would probably be closer to eighteen bucks American.)

The compound was a long circle drive with individual lean-to cabins each containing one bare lightbulb with a Mexican piruja (a Mexican woman who sells her body for money or things of value) standing by with a "come-hither look." There must have been ten or so of these little huts. One of the "girls" very closely resembled a large pigeon. Whoops, Jim Sullivan's fluency in Mexicali linguistics brought us to this very precarious situation.

He was apologetic and kept saying, "So sorry, guys."

Jim slipped the driver another $20, and we headed back to La Paz, where we dined in the relative safety of the hotel cantina!

Arriving back in St. Louis, I boasted to Susan about my world-record red snapper and my newly dubbed nickname, "El Magnifico." She said that she knew that that was a proper name for me even before we got married and said that it was a very appropriate title. (At least that is what I think she said.)

What Happens in
Port St. Lucie Doesn't
Stay in Port St. Lucie

In March 2008, I was with John Rooney again at spring training. Mike Shannon invited John to dinner that night to meet his newly found girlfriend, Lori Bergman (who later became Mrs. Shannon), and John asked me to tag along. I was thrilled at the opportunity, as a good meal at a fine restaurant is a difficult event for me to pass up. The restaurant was a white tablecloth restaurant with tuxedoed waiters, and the menu looked terrific.

The waiter came to the table to take our drink orders, and Mike Shannon asked me what I wanted.

I said, "Club soda, Mike."

He said, "Don't be shy. They have a terrific wine list. Just order what you want . . . I'm buying."

"Seriously, Mike, I drink no alcohol whatsoever. I have an allergy to it."

He pressed me further: "You can't be serious. You were a friend of Jack's (Jack Buck) and you don't drink at all?"

John Rooney chimed in and said, "No, Mike, Don doesn't drink alcohol at all."

I explained further: "Mike, I hate the taste of alcohol. I have no moral aversion to it. I just hate the taste, plus I get a shooting pain just above my eyebrows with just one taste and I feel nauseous. I see no reason to suffer through that."

He kept shaking his head, saying, "I can't believe it."

At any rate, my club soda was very refreshing and the meal was terrific. We ended the evening early because John and Mike were doing a Cardinals/Mets game in Port St. Lucie the next day and they both liked to arrive a couple of hours before the game.

John and I picked up Jim Jackson (the world-class broadcast engineer, and without Jim, there would be zero spring training broadcasts) and then picked up Mike Shannon, and we were on our way to Port St. Lucie for the game. It was really interesting to me because of conversations regarding compensation for pre- and post-game interviews . . . who does this and for-what pay. I was like a little fly on the wall hearing inside information that I never thought of before.

Before the game started, John Rooney and I were in a broadcast booth next to the visitor's booth when the national anthem started playing. John Rooney did a perfect Enrico Palazzo (Leslie Nielsen in *Naked Gun*) rendition of the anthem and had me laughing so hard that I almost teared up. Then he did a play-by-play of Porky Pig broadcasting a baseball game. That was the funniest broadcasting rendition of a pretend game that I ever heard. John could do stand-up comedy and bring down the house.

The game now is in progress and we are in the Cardinals (visitors) broadcast booth when Mike Shannon at the mike notices a "tiki hut" bar in the concourse in the left field stands and says something about it. I thought I heard my name, but then maybe not. I was to the left of John Rooney and one broadcast person away from Shannon. They both had headphones on and I didn't.

After the inning ends, Mike Shannon leans over past John Rooney and says to me, "Get ready for your phone to ring, big boy." (Mike's term of endearment for almost everyone.)

Several moments later, the phone rang, and it was my beautiful wife, Susan, listening to the broadcast in St. Louis, who said, "Well, what happens in Port St. Lucie doesn't stay in Port St. Lucie."

Mike Shannon, during the game, said, "There is our good friend, Don Marquess, in the tiki hut with a Bud Select in one hand and two tiki hut girls in the other hand."

When Mike gets on a subject, he doesn't let up easily. There were many more references to me being over there with the "beer and broads." He was having very hard time accepting my lifetime sobriety.

After saying those totally untrue things about me, he said to me, "I just made you a hero, big boy."

I thought Susan may be the only person listening to the broadcast who knew that it was a total fabrication.

From that time on, Don Marquess and the tiki hut adventure became a subject anytime a reference to the Mets in Port St. Lucie was brought up during any broadcast. Mike and his future wife, Lori, were in Key West and found a coconut that was very primitively carved in the shape of a hula dancer with a little grass skirt and bright red lips, which they brought to me as a gift because it was remindful of the tiki hut girls. It was mentioned numerous times during Cardinals broadcasts.

Susan, who was having as much fun with the tiki hut adventure as Mike and John were, found a photo on the internet of three oldish fat ladies in bikinis (super el yucko), had it printed, and enclosed it in an 8 ½ x 11 envelope with a note for Mike Shannon, saying, "Don has had so much fun with you and John talking about his "tiki hut" escapades. He is opening his own "tiki hut" in St. Louis. He put me in charge of hiring the waitresses. Here are my first choices. What do you think?"

OH DEER

St. Louis in 1991 had no casinos; however, directly across the
Missouri River in Alton, Illinois, a casino named the Alton Belle
had opened. It was a very small riverboat casino offering one-hour
cruises in order to comply with Illinois regulations. Our very close
friend, Lon Gilbert, who loved to gamble, had never been there; and
Susan and I offered to take him there in early October 1993. I might
also mention that I loved to play blackjack and didn't have to fly the
three-and-a-half-hour flight to Las Vegas to do so. This was to be
a fun evening . . .

St. Louis was settled as a major river port in 1764 and was at the
confluence of two major rivers: the Missouri and the Mississippi.
This was very wonderful for traders because pelts were transported
by boats from both the north by the Mississippi and the northwest
territories on the Missouri river. However, all of the water surging
together at the confluence of those rivers made that area susceptible
to periodic flooding. In 1993, St. Louis had a major flood, but the
highway to Alton was dry and clear; however, the adjacent area to
the highway was severely flooded. Traveling to the Alton Bridge
to enter the town that had the Alton Belle, the road, Highway 67,
was raised enough to be passable; however, both sides of the road
were nothing but trees and water, much like the cypress swamps
in southern Louisiana. There was a concrete median on Highway
67, and as we were traveling in the center lane next to this median,
a white truck slightly ahead of us in the curb lane swerved and

wobbled as if he had blown a tire. I looked at that truck for just a brief moment, and when I turned my vision back to my lane, there were three deer hopping and jumping in front of my car. It was dusk and my headlights were on, and the three deer in front of me looked like aliens in a Steven Spielberg movie, all three trying to get over the concrete median. In that very brief moment, I didn't know exactly what was behind me or to the side of my car, so I just slammed into them. One of the deer went over my car and his hoof damaged my trunk. One was completely smashed by my car. The third one escaped, and I assumed, unharmed. The hood and front bumper of my 1992 white Lexus ES300 was smooshed and very bloody. I called the highway patrol, and a car with a trooper arrived in a few minutes.

I explained in detail to the trooper how it happened, and he said that that happens with regularity with deer trying to escape the flooding. However, to get three at a time hadn't happened before. Susan, my beautiful wife, who was the nurturing mother of all living creatures, was crying about the death of those deer.

The officer said, "Ma'am, your husband saved your life. Many drivers slam on their brakes and are hit from behind by another car, or swerve into a different lane and cause a major collision. Your husband did the right thing and saved your life." (The more he spoke, the taller I got.)

I became the heroic driver of the month in my mind and just felt great that he said all of those great things to my wife. I really felt bad about hitting and killing them also; however, I also felt pretty horrible about the damage to my Lexus, knowing fully well that those deer had no liability insurance (the repair bill was $6,700). I told the trooper that the deer were his if he wanted them. He said he did and thanked me.

We never made it to the Alton Belle that evening, but I did get a couple of bucks regardless. (Sorry about that.)

THE CARTIER WATCH

In my years as an architectural representative for my father's brick company, I developed many friendships with architects in the area. Two of my very good friends, Frank Riedman and Tom Wilkins, formed a new architectural firm named Wilkins Riedman Architects. Tom and Frank had worked together on many projects including the Anheuser-Busch corporate headquarters. Their first project together was the St. Louis Soccer Park. Frank Riedman had always loved Cartier watches and purchased one to celebrate their new project.

Frank and I had become close friends, and he told me this credible story.

Frank was driving a prospective client to look at a building that the new client admired at the University of Missouri's School of Mining and Metallurgy located in Rolla, Missouri, which is located around one hundred miles southwest of St. Louis, about a two-hour drive. Frank and the new client were deep in discussion regarding the new project when Frank took off his new Cartier watch, wound it (this was in the seventies, and his watch had to be wound, no battery involved), and after winding it, unrolled his window, and threw his watch out the window. Frank smoked, and looked in the ash tray and saw his cigarette in the tray. Apparently, he was so deep in discussion with his new client that he had a momentary brain freeze and thought he was throwing his cigarette out the window. Frank was mortified and pulled off the interstate at the next exit ramp.

The client asked, "Why are we pulling off the highway?"

Frank said, "I accidentally threw something out the window."

The client asked, "What did you throw out?"

Frank, trying to avoid admitting his momentary stupidity, especially in front of his new client, thought for a few moments, and said, not wanting to lie to the client, "I threw my brand-new Cartier watch out the window about a mile back!"

"What? You threw your watch out the window? How in the hell did you do that?"

Frank replied, "I have no idea. I guess I thought I was throwing my cigarette away, and I was so engrossed about your new building, I guess I had a momentary brain freeze."

The client was speechless.

They searched and searched, but never found his watch. Surprisingly, Frank got the new project with the client, who told Frank that that story was worth every bit of his design fee.